DEVIL'S ADVOCATES

DEVIL'S ADVOCATES is a series of books devoted to exploring the classics of horror cinema. Contributors to the series come from the fields of teaching, academia, journalism and fiction, but all have one thing in common: a passion for the horror film and a desire to share it with the widest possible audience.

'The admirable Devil's Advocates series is not only essential – and fun – reading for the serious horror fan but should be set texts on any genre course.'
Dr Ian Hunter, Reader in Film Studies, De Montfort University, Leicester

'Auteur Publishing's new Devil's Advocates critiques on individual titles... offer bracingly fresh perspectives from passionate writers. The series will perfectly complement the BFI archive volumes.' **Christopher Fowler,** *Independent on Sunday*

'Devil's Advocates has proven itself more than capable of producing impassioned, intelligent analyses of genre cinema... quickly becoming the go-to guys for intelligent, easily digestible film criticism.' *Horror Talk.com*

'Auteur Publishing continue the good work of giving serious critical attention to significant horror films.' *Black Static*

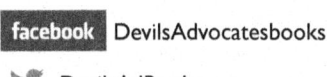 DevilsAdvocatesbooks

DevilsAdBooks

DEVIL'S ADVOCATES

MACBETH

REBEKAH OWENS

Acknowledgments

Thanks are due to John Atkinson at Auteur for giving me the opportunity to write about this great film, and for his editorial assistance. Thank you also to Karin Brown of the Shakespeare Institute Library, University of Birmingham, for supplying materials above and beyond the call of duty for any Librarian; to Dr Sue Knott for reading and checking the various drafts; and to Andrew Anderson for sharing some ideas about Folk Horror. It is to him this book is dedicated.

First published in 2017 by
Auteur, 24 Hartwell Crescent, Leighton Buzzard LU7 1NP
www.auteur.co.uk
Copyright © Auteur 2017

Series design: Nikki Hamlett at Cassels Design
Set by Cassels Design www.casselsdesign.co.uk
Printed and bound in Great Britain

British Library Cataloguing-in-Publication Data
A catalogue record for this book is available from the British Library

ISBN paperback: 978-1-911325-13-0
ISBN ebook: 978-1-911325-14-7

CONTENTS

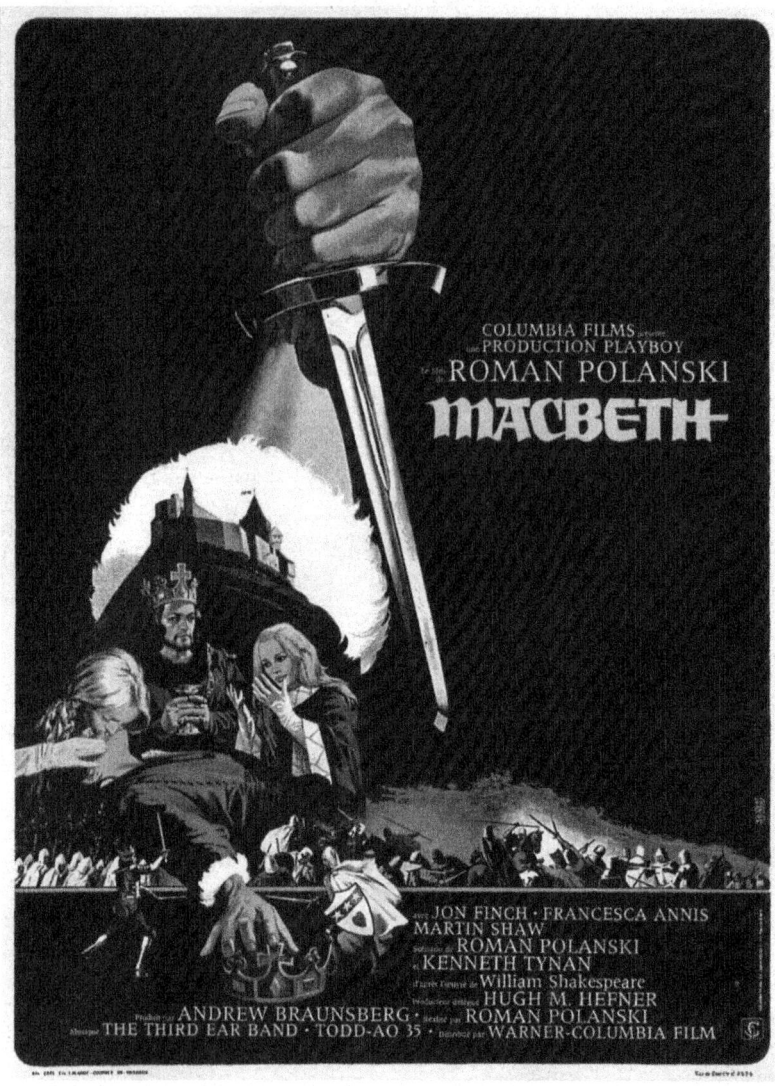

Theatrical release poster for *Macbeth*.

SHAKESPEARE'S *MACBETH* – 'THIS MOST BLOODY PIECE OF WORK'

Fig. 1. Illustration from title page of the 1615 edition of Thomas Kyd's *The Spanish Tragedy*.

When William Shakespeare wrote *Macbeth*, he was already a successful playwright with some 28 plays behind him. He was working at the Globe in London, in the commercial environment of a professional theatre. His individual working practices are generally unknown, but in the Elizabethan and Jacobean theatre the work ethic was that of collaboration, of a co-operative of fellow playwrights who wrote for the stage.

Many of this group of writers produced plays with features we would recognise today as 'horror'. Although such a genre did not exist *per se*, playgoers to the early modern theatre would have seen a fair proportion of plays that contained constituents of horror. One such play was popular for the best part of thirty years, a drama called *The Spanish Tragedy*, written around 1587, by the prolific playwright, Thomas Kyd. Inspired by the Roman dramatist Seneca, whose tragedies were the forerunners of many plays involving revenge-fuelled slaughter, Kyd's play opens with a ghost called Don Andrea describing how he died and what happened to him in the afterlife. He observes the events as they unfold on the stage, which includes witnessing one of the most memorable scenes in the play. This involves a father's discovery of his son's hanged and disembowelled body in his garden, a killing which the audience have seen and which has happened in front of the victim's horrified lover. One of the perpetrators of the murder is killed, one hanged for the crime. The finale of the play has multiple deaths, including two murders, a suicide and the main character, Hieronimo, biting out his own tongue on the stage.

These are recognisable features of what we think of now as 'slasher' style horror – though it should again be emphasised that no such genre existed at the time – and such features do show that the presence of violence and blood in drama has obviously entertained audiences for a long time. The Spanish Tragedy shows that we can trace many aspects of the modern horror film to the early theatre. Christopher Marlowe's Dr Faustus, first published in 1604, contains another familiar modern horror trope, that of the supernatural. Borrowing from the English Medieval Morality tradition, the play concerns the world of demons and gods, involving a deal with the devil, the Seven Deadly Sins, a Good and Bad Angel and an ending in which the protagonist is dragged into hell through a large prop 'hell mouth' constructed on the stage.

Props such as these provided the early version of horror 'special effects'. To stage George Peele's The Battle of Alcazar (published in 1594) required the use of a sheep's bladder stuffed with the animal's lungs, heart and liver for the staged disembowelling of three characters. That most recognisable of horror icons, the skull, is a ubiquitous prop in the more grisly Jacobean dramas. In The Revenger's Tragedy (attr. Thomas Middleton, 1606), a bereaved lover Vindice takes his revenge on a murderer by coating the skull of his former lover with poison and persuading her killer to kiss it.

One of Shakespeare's colleagues developed so prominent a reputation as an author of horror that he has since been immortalised as such in popular culture. John Webster is portrayed by Joe Roberts in Shakespeare In Love as the child tormenting a mouse and uttering lines such as 'I liked it when she stabbed herself'. He wrote The White Devil (1612), featuring a professional hitman, a poisoned painting and helmet, neck-snapping, strangulation and multiple stabbings. Around a year later, he created The Duchess of Malfi, a work that features a prototype werewolf in the character of the lycanthropic Ferdinand.

Shakespeare was himself the author of a 'horror' play. One of his first works was Titus Andronicus (1594). This play has a description of human sacrifice at the beginning, in which someone is diced (offstage) and thrown on a funeral pyre. The mother of the victim, Tamora, Queen of the Goths, plots revenge for this act on the daughter of the man behind the sacrifice, Titus Andronicus. This takes the form of the rape and mutilation of his beloved child Lavinia – she has her hands hacked off and her tongue sliced out by Tamora's sons, Chiron and Demetrius. This act, too, requires avenging and leads to the famous dénouement in which the perpetrators of the rape are killed by Titus and baked in a pie which their mother unwittingly eats.[1]

Such is the violence of this play that one critic catalogued ' ... 14 killings, 9 of them on stage, 6 severed members, 1 rape ... 1 live burial ... and ... cannibalism [that makes for] an average of 5.2 atrocities per act, or one for every 97 lines' (Hulse, 1979: 106). It is a list of horrors worthy of the modern slasher. Shakespeare's later works did not involve quite so much bloodshed; but he did still include supernatural elements such as ghosts – most famously in *Hamlet* (1600) – and other motifs that would, eventually, combine with these gory elements to form a recognised genre in both literature and film.

SYNOPSIS

When he wrote *Macbeth* in 1606, Shakespeare drew on the existing traditions of folklore and superstition to create a play with witches, ghosts and prophecies. The story of the play concerns Macbeth, the Thane of Glamis, defeating an invading army and securing a victory for Duncan, King of Scotland. Returning from the battle, Macbeth and his friend Banquo meet three women, who purport to be witches. They tell Macbeth that he will be promoted to Thane of Cawdor and ultimately become king. Banquo is told that he will not be a king himself, but his descendants will rule Scotland for many generations. When Macbeth is given the title of Thane of Cawdor, he begins to brood on the witches' prediction of his further promotion. He writes to his wife, who determines that such a promotion should be precipitated and tells her husband that, when Duncan comes to stay with them, he should die. She persuades Macbeth to murder the king and conspires with him to lay the blame elsewhere.

After the murder, Macbeth is crowned King of Scotland. The king's sons, Malcolm and Donalbain, flee the country, accused of the murder of their father. Feeling far from secure, Macbeth finds that he is haunted by the prophecy that Banquo will be the one who creates a royal dynasty and not himself. He arranges the murder of Banquo and his son, Fleance. The latter escapes death, but his father is brutally murdered. Macbeth is satisfied that he is secure on the throne.

At the feast on the same night, Macbeth sees Banquo's ghost. It unnerves him so much, he visits the witches in their lair to find out what the future holds for him as king. He is told by a succession of spirits and ghosts that he can only be killed when the forest of Birnam Wood moves toward Dunsinane castle and that he cannot die except by the hand of one who is not born of woman. Relieved, Macbeth decides to act on a further warning from the weird sisters that he should 'beware the Thane of Fife' (4.1.86), a man called Macduff. On discovering that the Thane of Fife has defected to England, Macbeth arranges for the murder of his wife and children. When Macduff learns of this, he has already joined the English army led by Malcolm, and the news of his family's murder redoubles his resolve to challenge Macbeth's tyranny. In the meantime, Lady Macbeth has been sleepwalking, talking of the murder of Duncan, Macduff's wife and Banquo and miming washing blood off her hands. In her guilt, she commits suicide. Macbeth does not allow this to shake his faith and he prepares for battle, taking refuge in the witches' prophecies of his invincibility. When he is told that it appears as if the forest at Birnam is approaching the castle, he becomes afraid; and when he learns that Macduff was not born of woman but was 'untimely ripped' (5.7.46) from his mother's womb, he realises that he is defeated. Nevertheless, he fights on ('Lay on, Macduff': 5.7.63), and is killed. The play ends with the beheading of Macbeth and the new king Malcolm's wise words on his impending benevolent rule.

*

The fact that the play caught the popular imagination as a work that dealt with the supernatural can be seen in the changes that were made to it by another playwright. Early modern theatre was a commercial enterprise, as well as a collaborative one. Unlike today, authors did not have the copyright of their work. Plays were not the sole property of their authors, but of the theatre. This meant that whenever they were restaged or revived they were sometimes updated or changed to suit the demands of the audience or of a different venue, and such revisions were not necessarily performed by the original author. In the case of *Macbeth*, when Shakespeare had first written the work, it was performed in the open air of the Globe Theatre in London. When, in around 1608/9, the Kings' Men, Shakespeare's company, took over another property, the Blackfriars Theatre, they acquired an indoor venue. This meant that a play like *Macbeth* could be adjusted to suit such a theatre since the scope for what we would now call 'special effects' would be greatly improved. To take advantage of this, another playwright, Thomas Middleton, added songs and dances to Macbeth's final encounter with the witches. What had originally been a stark confrontation between Macbeth, the weird women and spirits became a Chorus involving the goddess Hecate and some extra witches, and songs which Middleton also used for his own play, *The Witch*.[2]

The fact that Shakespeare's play acquired more supernatural elements over the years indicates that, as time went on *Macbeth* had become synonymous with such things. It acquired all the ingredients that would, in the future, be associated with modern film horror (even the songs, as any admirer of *Little Shop of Horrors* [1986] will testify). It also had another aspect that we would associate with modern horror – topical relevance. Sara M. Deats has explored the play's historical context. She noted that 'The ascension to the English throne in 1603 of the Scottish monarch James I, a direct descendant of Banquo' probably motivated Shakespeare to write a play on the subject of Scotland and its kings. In addition, King James was obsessed with witchcraft. He had written a book in 1599 entitled *Daemonologie*. In this work, which takes as read that witches are real, James outlined the correct way of dealing with them, becoming a defender of the practice of witch-hunting. Given this, and the fresh memories of the Gunpowder Plot in 1605 that involved the potential murder of a king, Deats considered the play as 'a dramatic manifestation of a particular historical moment' (1986: 84).

Given that Shakespeare's *Macbeth* not only deals with the supernatural, but also has the scope to be regarded as a commentary on contemporary thinking, it is no surprise that any modern director would choose that particular play to make into a horror film, since such a combination would allow them to use Shakespeare's text to create horror effects that would appeal to a mass cinema audience, whilst using Shakespeare's universality to make points about current social and political issues.

Two notable directors were attracted by *Macbeth* before Roman Polanski. Orson Welles' 1948 film is based upon his stage production, the so-called 'voodoo *Macbeth*', which incorporated African-American culture. Both play and its reception were 'fraught with contemporary political realities' (Kliman, 2004: 121). In the 1936 production, for example, there were only two professional black actors in the cast due to the 'scant opportunities in legitimate theatre' (2004: 113) offered for black performers at that time. Welles' film, made 12 years later, still used the play to reflect contemporary political concerns. In its post-war context, it has been seen as 'a parable of fascism narrowly averted' (Pearlman, 1995: 252).

The Japanese *auteur,* Akira Kurosawa filmed the story as *Kumonosu-Jô,* commonly known as *Throne of Blood* (also known as *The Castle of the Spider's Web*) in 1957. This version of the play is described as a '"transformation" rather than an adaptation of *Macbeth*' (Rothwell, 2004: 182) and borrows both from Japanese Noh Theatre and the Western, presenting the story as a meditation on the 'corruption at the heart of [a] society' (Kliman, 2004:186), that tolerates crimes that go against the moral order of nature.[3]

Though they use *Macbeth* to express political concerns, neither Welles nor Kurosawa interpret the play's supernatural elements using the conventions of the horror film, by then an established film genre. Two reasons for this. One is that by the time of Welles' film, horror as a genre had become blurred with science fiction. From the boom in horror films of the early 1930s, by the 1940s, audiences were watching films that contained horror elements – monsters and suspense – but which were exploiting sci-fi elements – space travel and atomic bombs – to provide social commentary in films such as *The Day The Earth Stood Still* (1951). In the second instance, while contemporary concerns provided plenty of scope for interpretation of Shakespeare, the presentation of horror itself tended to rely on source material from the more recent literary historical sources. *The Curse of Frankenstein* in 1957, released the same year as *Throne of Blood,* was a Hammer horror that commandeered, via Universal Studios, the Gothic novel as its source, looking to the literary horror classics of the nineteenth century for its inspiration rather than Elizabethan and Jacobean plays, however gory they may be.

It is for these reasons that, though both Welles and Kurosawa included the supernatural elements of the play, the witches and the ghosts, neither director exploited their presence to infuse the film as a whole. Both films are principally explorations of Shakespeare's play as the story of a tormented individual (in Welles' case) or the dangers of overreaching ambition (Kurosawa) presented in highly stylised expressionistic settings. There was only one director who embraced the idea of horror as a medium for the full expression of Shakespeare's *Macbeth*.

FOOTNOTES

1.   See the film version directed by Julie Taymor starring Anthony (Hannibal the Cannibal) Hopkins as Titus (1999).

2.   See William Shakespeare. *Macbeth*. Ed. Nicholas Brooke. World's Classics Series. Oxford: OUP, 1994: 34-5. All subsequent references to Shakespeare's play will be from this edition and quotations from the film will be marked with the corresponding reference in the text. See also *Thomas Middleton: The Collected Works*. Eds. Gary Taylor and John Lavagnino. Oxford: Clarendon Press, 2007: 1165-7.

3.   For a detailed account of both films see Kliman (2004) 183-90 for Kurosawa and 122-27 for Welles. See also the accounts of both films in Rothwell (2004) at 70-4 (Welles) and 185-88 (Kurosawa).

CHAPTER 1: POLANSKI AND HORROR: *ROSEMARY'S BABY*

Fig. 2. Rosemary sees inside the crib (eyes of the devil superimposed either side of mother).

In order to appreciate *Macbeth* as a horror film, it is worth considering how Roman Polanski approached the genre, by a consideration of his horror output before that film. He was hardly new to the genre when he decided to make a film of *Macbeth*. His 1965 work *Repulsion* centres around Carol Ledoux (played by Catherine Deneuve) and her disintegrating sanity, expressed from her subjective viewpoint. With walls that crack, hands that reach out, changing camera perspectives and a hypnotic mind-numbing soundtrack of repetitive sounds, the film is more in the realms of a psychological thriller than overtly horror. These are brutal murders; but the emphasis in *Repulsion* is on the mind, on its ability to distort the reality around it.

Repulsion showed Polanski to be a master of the craft of psychological horror; but his early attempt at a more overtly Gothic horror was not so successful. That he was not unaware of the more Gothic aspects of the genre is recorded in his autobiography. He wrote of his experiences watching horror films in Paris, noticing that in the cinemas, the 'audiences were reduced to laughter' (1984: 212). This was his reference to the British Hammer films that had been in vogue during the late 1950s and 1960s but, by the end of the decade were declining in popularity – and quality. The films, as Polanski had himself here observed, had become so hackneyed and clichéd that they were laughable. Production values in these films had declined. Polanski wrote of the 'tatty rural location situated conveniently near a film studio' (ibid.), a reference to the home of the Hammer film studios at Down Place (Bray Studios) on the Thames, the house and grounds that provided many locations for the films. Such a location symbolised for him the over-familiarity of the Hammer style, now as 'tatty' as the property itself.[1]

Polanski seized upon this view of the old and decided to make it new. Seeing the juxtaposition of horror and laughter, he decided to make a horror film that was *designed* to make people laugh, rather than the unintentional merriment that Hammer horror had provoked. He had the idea of writing a 'vampire spoof', a horror film that an audience 'could laugh with, rather than at', reimagining many of the motifs of film horror that were causing the audiences such mirth (ibid.).

The resulting film was a combination of Hammer motifs and modern comic sensibilities. The story takes place in a familiar horror location – Transylvania – and has two stalwarts of the Hammer tradition as its central characters – a Professor, Abronsius (Jack MacGowran) and an apprentice, Alfred (played by Polanski himself). They are vampire hunters and attempt to rescue an innkeeper (Alfie Bass) and his daughter (Sharon Tate) from the vampire, Count Von Krolock (Ferdy Mayne, made up to resemble Christopher Lee as Dracula). As expected, this senior vampire has the correct aristocratic manner, lives in a suitably sinister castle, in a snowy, isolated setting and has his needs met by a hunchbacked servant. Interspersed with the action are the jokes, such as Bass' Jewish vampire who mocks attempts to ward him off with a cross.

Despite his best efforts in making *The Fearless Vampire Killers* (1967; released in the UK as *Dance of the Vampires*) the result was not successful. This was not down to the fact that Polanski had made a bad horror film, but that the studio management had misunderstood his intentions. When the film was released, Polanski realised he had made a mistake by allowing producer Martin Ransohoff to have the final edit on behalf of the distributors MGM (Polanski, 1984: 237). It was redubbed with the voices of American actors, shortened by 20 minutes and gained an animated prologue. It was also given the crass subtitle 'Pardon me, but your teeth are in my neck', a phrase which thoroughly undermines the delicate balance of comedy and horror conventions Polanski was attempting by its verbal echoes of the British *Carry On* farces. The result was so unsatisfactory that Polanski tried to distance himself from it.

If nothing else, Polanski's reaction to someone else (mis)handling his work underlines the artistic credentials for which he was to become known. That he tried to have his name taken off the credits because the finished product did not resemble his own vision reflects his insistence upon the integrity of his own artistry. As far as he possibly could in all of his subsequent work, including *Macbeth*, all aspects of filmmaking were subordinate to that vision, be they material concerns such as props and make-up or budgets. Such a vision mattered, even to the point of compromised relationships with financial backers, heads of studios, production crews and the actors themselves, all of whom he expected to be suborned to his creative control.[2]

Given such unwavering self-belief in his artistic credibility, it is no wonder Polanski tried to disown *The Fearless Vampire Killers*, and it might seem that the compromised version released can tell us little about Polanski's approach to *Macbeth*. It was not initially a commercial success, and on its release gave the impression that Polanski had relied on a (sometimes crass) evocation of all the clichés of the genre. It was seen as a complete contrast to the aesthetic qualities of *Repulsion* and that film's expression of horror as tied to the human condition.

There have, however, since been more sensitive reappraisals of the work, especially given that Polanski was eventually able to release his own version of it.[3] This film is now seen as containing a burgeoning filmic 'vocabulary' for Polanskian horror: 'The juxtaposition of the extraordinary and the trivial, the horrific and the funny in *Dance of the Vampires* ... prefigures *Macbeth* and later horror films by this director' (Mazierska, 2007: 170). In addition, for my purpose here, what this film shows, is that Polanski was beginning to form the ideas that would shape his interpretation of *Macbeth* as a horror film. In *Vampire Killers*, we see the director starting to muse upon the form, and experiment with it as a medium for his artistic expression. It is an important film in Polanski's horror canon, in that it tells us a great deal about these early reflections. He knew that what he had witnessed in the Paris audience was evidence of a genre in transition; and the decision to make a 'spoof' or a parody indicates a close intellectual engagement with the material. In order to parody anything, it is essential to have a full understanding of that which is being parodied. For Polanski to decide to make a 'spoof' of a vampire film, he needed to have an understanding of what elements constituted such a film; and he realised that those elements could be reconfigured into something entirely new. This was also the basis for his next film, *Rosemary's Baby* (1968), a film that had a direct impact on his realisation of *Macbeth*.

ROSEMARY'S BABY – 'THERE ARE NO WITCHES, NOT REALLY'

The best model of a Polanskian horror before *Macbeth* was *Rosemary's Baby*. This was (and remains) his best known and most commercially successful horror film. Part of the reason for its success was because it represented a maturation of Polanski's style with regard to the genre. In this film, he successfully matched the expectations of the old format of the horror film, using the Hammer horror, Gothic tradition and grafted upon it a new, modern, dimension.

In this discussion of *Rosemary's Baby*, it can be seen how Polanski used the older horror conventions and fused them with the new in a way that would have repercussions for his film of *Macbeth*. These are: the subjective viewpoint of the protagonist; the belief in the supernatural with no evidence presented that such a thing exists; and the revelation that there is no supernatural agency on which to blame the evils perpetuated by humans.

Rosemary's Baby was the first of Polanski's films to be based upon a literary source, in this case a novel by Ira Levin. Robert Evans, then the vice-president of Paramount, handed Polanski the galley proofs of Levin's novel, knowing that the subject matter would appeal to the young artist. Initially dismissing the novel as a 'soap opera' from its first pages, Polanski read the rest, in his own words with his eyes 'popping out of [his] head' (1984: 225), a suitably grisly metaphor for the book's subject matter of covens, demonic rituals and Satanism.

The story involves a young couple, Rosemary (Mia Farrow) and Guy Woodhouse (John Cassavetes), who move into their dream apartment in New York, where they can pursue their ambitions – his of an acting career and hers of starting a family. Despite being warned off, they move into the Bramford Building, rumoured to have been the site of black magic rituals and the summoning of Satan. On meeting their elderly neighbours, Minnie and Roman Castevet (Ruth Gordon and Sidney Blackmer), Rosemary becomes an unwilling victim of their black magic practices, and is impregnated, she believes, with the son of Satan at their – and her husband's – instigation.

At first, it might seem that this film has very little to do with Polanski's subsequent film of *Macbeth*. From this outline of the plot, they could hardly seem more different. One is based on a modern novel, one on a Jacobean drama. The visuals of both films seem to have nothing in common. *Rosemary's Baby* is set in twentieth-century New York, a definitively urban milieu; *Macbeth* in the rustic landscapes of Medieval Scotland. Even the soundtracks are very different. The dialogue in *Rosemary's Baby* is modern, New York/American vernacular as opposed to Shakespearean early modern poetry and prose. The NY-based film has the sounds of a familiar modernity – of traffic, wailing sirens, ringing telephones, the voice of the television and the music of the record player. In *Macbeth*, the soundtrack is Renaissance-style music augmented by the noises of nature – birds calling, horses galloping, thunder rumbling. Even the commonalities between the two films are, at first sight, very superficial: covens of naked witches, the sounds of chanting and the control of someone by supernatural means.

The connection between the two films is not to be found by such a summary of the superficial features, however. It goes to the very core of *Rosemary's Baby*, to the foundational idea that infuses the film. The connection between the two works becomes clear in a consideration of Polanski's concept of the film and how that concept is realised; namely, how has he portrayed the supernatural? To identify this gives us a clearer picture of the themes that constitute his approach to horror in *Rosemary's Baby*, which can then lead to an instructive reappraisal of *Macbeth* in the light of the horror genre.

In the first instance, Polanski deviated from his literary source in *Rosemary's Baby* in one crucial aspect. As he explained in his autobiography, Levin's novel is concerned with Satanism and the reader is left in no doubt that what happens to Rosemary is the result of occult practices. As an agnostic, as one who believed in neither God or Satan, Polanski 'decided that there would have to be a loophole – the possibility that Rosemary's supernatural experiences were figments of her imagination' (1984: 228). To that end, he set about creating a deliberate ambiguity in the film. He organised the material in such a way that it could be interpreted by an audience as a story about Rosemary's isolation and growing paranoia, rather than as a story of a vulnerable young woman at the hands of an evil cult.

This is in keeping with Polanski at his best, as a filmmaker who depicts states of mind. He wanted, as he wrote in his autobiography 'to adopt the same subjective approach to the theme as … *Repulsion*' (1984: 234). He was influenced in this respect by a book called *Eye and Brain: The Psychology of Seeing* by R. L. Gregory (1984: 235). This had been published in 1966 and was a scientific analysis of perception, of how the senses work. Of particular interest to Polanski was Gregory's work on vision. He had proposed that what we actually see in front of us is influenced by many factors, especially memory, all of which can serve to obscure or affect the reality taken in by our eyes.

Polanski translated Gregory's work literally on the screen by the use of camera angles to act as the 'eyes' of the protagonist, Rosemary. He had a working knowledge of the technical effects that would be needed to achieve this, such as using a short focal lens that enabled him to convey a 'subjective immediacy' (1984: 234) using camera effects to deceive the eye of the audience.[4] In this way, he could tell the story entirely through Rosemary's eyes, creating a film based on her subjective vision. That he considered he had achieved his aim is expressed in an anecdote from the film's early release. As Polanski reported, he successfully affected the audience's perception of the film as a whole:

> Many people emerged from theaters convinced that [in the final scene] they'd seen the baby, cloven hooves and all. In fact, all they'd really seen, for a split second, was a subliminal superimposition of the catlike eyes that glare down at Rosemary during her nightmare in the early part of the film. (1984: 235)

He had so successfully altered the perceptions of the audience that they saw something that was not there.[5] This idea that reality could be interpreted by the preoccupations of the observer was to have a powerful influence on *Macbeth*.

In *Rosemary's Baby*, the concept is fully explored by having the narrative told entirely from Rosemary's point of view. It is she whom the camera follows and it is her experiences that we share. To this effect Polanski compromised on the woman he chose for the role, eschewing the image of 'a robust, healthy, all-American girl' (1984: 231) for the slenderness of Mia Farrow, whose 'delicate quality' he felt, 'would project vulnerability' (Zinoman, 2011: 21). Those qualities are augmented in the film by Farrow's costume – light shift dresses with Peter Pan collars that subliminally accentuate her youth and innocence. She changes her hair to a short cut by Vidal Sassoon that serves to frame her face and emphasise her suffering as it is reflected in her small features. Farrow's slim frame and large eyes allow the audience to see that vulnerability, and be lulled into empathy by that same fragility. It is her we follow throughout the film and what she feels, we feel: her irritation at the Castevets, the hurtful neglect of her, increasingly, mysteriously successful husband.

Once we have this rapport with Rosemary, we then share her fears. Although delighted by her pregnancy, she becomes increasingly paranoid. Her suffering is shared and invites empathy. She has severe stomach pains, and in one particularly striking shot, we see Rosemary doubled up on a seat in front of the television, oblivious to its noise, absorbed in her own silent world of pain. The subdued light, the muted sound, creates an external image of her inner suffering by which we are moved. By the time she begins to articulate her belief that what is happening to her is being caused by someone else, we have been persuaded entirely to believe her: to believe that the chocolate mousse tastes chalky, that mould or fungus can have magical properties, that items of clothing can be used in charms or spells to debilitate or kill people. As she expresses her fears to others, we see in her face the hurt when she is disbelieved and that gives us cause to think there might really be something going on. When her friend Hutch (Maurice Evans) does the research and comes up with an answer, we know the relief that she feels at finally having such answers – no matter how absurd. Her final meeting with Dr Hill (Charles Grodin) as she pours out her conviction that she is the victim of a coven of witches who have killed to achieve their ends is strikingly achieved. We should be watching Dr Hill and his growing disbelief and concern for her welfare, his reaction when he asks to see the book on witchcraft Rosemary has been reading. Instead, we feel happy for Rosemary – that she seems to have escaped and will be safe. At the end, when she has been captured and returned to the Bramford, we see her reaction to the child in the crib and we believe, because she does, that she has given birth to the Antichrist.

This is the masterstroke by Polanski. We have empathised with Rosemary so strongly at this point that, like the audiences leaving the cinema during its first screenings, we are convinced that we can see she has been used as a vessel to give birth to a son of Satan. Our perception of events has been cleverly manipulated and we see what Polanski wants us to see: a woman who thinks she has been manipulated by evil forces.

The point is, as the agnostic director proposed, there are no evil forces. She has not been the object of supernatural influence. What Polanski has portrayed is the power of the *belief* in the supernatural. This is an approach that would have a direct influence on *Macbeth*. This idea that there are no numinous forces that can influence and control human affairs appears as a subliminal theme in *Rosemary's Baby*. Polanski presents Rosemary herself as having lapsed in her own Catholic beliefs ('I was brought up a Catholic, now I don't know'). There is the appearance of the notorious 1966 issue of *Time* magazine fronted by the 'Is God Dead?' headline in the office of Dr. Sapirstein; and when Rosemary is using a set of Scrabble tiles to resolve what she is told is an anagram of 'Steven Marcato', one of the possible solutions she devises is the phrase 'How is hell fact..?'

This relates to the overt theme in the film that, despite any doubts, or lack of evidence, people still believe in God, or gods. Rosemary is clearly still influenced by her upbringing, shown in the film by her obvious discomfort when the Castevets start criticising the Pope. The film explores what happens when people have a stronger faith and act according to its precepts, no matter what the consequences. This idea is more explicitly realised in the character of Guy Woodhouse, Rosemary's husband.

Guy's faith is in himself, in his acting abilities and that, because of this talent, he is destined for greatness. In the film, he is initially struggling actor, disappointed with his career of minor plays and television commercials. He is distraught when he fails to obtain a key role in a play, one that would boost his career. His disappointment stems from his strong sense of entitlement, as seen in the passing remarks he makes in judgement about others, such as the comment that Rosemary's choice of Dr Hill is wrong since he is a 'Charlie nobody', unlike the Castevets' choice, Dr Sapirstein, who treats New York's elite. We pay little attention to Guy – partly because we are encouraged to focus on Rosemary, but mainly because we never see him working as an actor, apart from some occasional rehearsals with a pair of crutches. Polanski is careful not to associate him with any other actors against whom he may be judged, or to place him in the context of any theatre. He shot but cut a scene where Rosemary goes to see *The Fantasticks* and which included a cameo from Joan Crawford, so no real theatre or 'real' actors intrude in the action. We never see Guy in conversation with a fellow performer; he hears the news of Donald Baumgart's sudden blindness and subsequent departure from a major theatrical role from someone else. This has the effect of distancing Guy from the theatre and removing any objective judgement we might have of his merits as a performer. It means that information regarding his talents and abilities only comes from Guy himself. His overly enthusiastic response to Roman Castevet's praise of his performance in a play illustrates his readiness to believe in his own talents. All that matters in the film is the faith Guy has in himself: and he clearly considers that he is someone who has a destiny.

This is a suitable motivation for his agreeing to what the Castevets propose. That, in return, for the use of Rosemary's womb, they will further his career. It could be seen that, in agreeing to this, he is another vulnerable character preyed on by an evil cult and is just as exploited as Rosemary. He does, after all, encounter a coven of witches who promise him greatness, and perhaps he, too, is lured by their magic into striking a bargain with them. However, if there are no supernatural elements in the film and no magic, if Rosemary is deluded as to their existence, then so is Guy. Remove that otherworldly motivation and all you are left with is a man who is very ordinary, but very ambitious. So much so, that he is prepared to pursue his own desires at the expense of everyone else – even his own wife. This idea that, at the heart of everything, there are only human desires that motivate evil acts, is central to *Macbeth*.

In fairness, it could be reasonably argued that Polanski fails. That there is no ambiguity regarding the presence of the supernatural in the film, since the Castevets are very clearly attempting to influence events (see Newman, 2011: 57-8). Rosemary's reaction to her child, the horror she expresses at its appearance at the end of the film, could be interpreted as a confirmation of her conviction that she has been a victim of Satanic magic. Along with the Castevets' cries of 'Hail, Satan!' and their firm belief that the baby in the black-clothed crib is the son of the Devil it could be said that by the film's end Polanski had resolved any ambiguities by proving in the end that Rosemary was right.

However, *belief* is the operative word. If this is a film about the belief in the supernatural, and not an account of its tangible existence, it is worth having a closer look at the ending. It is the climax of the presentation throughout of how the Castevets are portrayed. A consideration of their role reveals that the ending endorses Polanski's central idea, not contradicts it.

As with everything else, the Castevets are only ever seen through Rosemary's eyes. They are elderly and much is made of this by Rosemary, as when she organises the party where 'you have to be under sixty to get in'. They are presented through her, as a stereotypical elderly couple: they live in an apartment where they fuss over spillages, Minnie knits, goes Christmas shopping, is prone to malapropisms – she mispronounces 'mousse' comically as 'mouse' – even nags and rebukes her husband in conversations overheard by Rosemary through the thin partition wall.

Though the Castevets are presented as a slightly comical couple, through Rosemary we suspect they may be witches. Yet at no point do we see the Castevets doing what she claims they do. We do not see Minnie Castevet add anything to the chocolate mousse, we do not see her mix the herbal drink. It *might* be tannis root in the necklace but we have not seen it being prepared. The only time we see the Castevets practising Satanism is when we share Rosemary's vision of them, naked and chanting in a ritual: but Polanski is careful never to offer us any empirical evidence that, as practising devil worshippers, the Castevets can influence events. Nowhere in the film are we offered such undisputable precepts. There is only their *belief* that what they are doing works. All the conversations that we overhear, via Rosemary ('Sometimes I wonder how come you're the leader of anything!') and the sounds and sights of them performing the ritual only indicate the depth of their belief. As to the efficacy of those beliefs, there is no evidence.

This is particularly well-expressed in the final moments of the film. When Rosemary approaches the crib and looks in, she cries 'What have you done to it? What have you done to its eyes?' But we do not see what she has seen. The camera remains on Rosemary. The only impression we receive, the one that so memorably deceived the audiences, is the fleeting impression of the yellow eyes she saw in her vision. We make the connection between that vision and her fearful remark subliminally – but we have not seen it. The only information we have that this is a son of Satan comes from not just

Fig. 3. Rosemary's reaction to the child that we do not see, dictates our own response.

Rosemary, but the reaction of the Castevets. In much of this final scene, we hear them and their guests praising Satan and his son. We hear that they have named the child Adrian, after Roman Castevet's father – again, we form a subliminal connection, this time with the man who was rumoured to have raised Satan himself in the very same building. We hear the Biblical-sounding prophecies about him, overthrowing the mighty and laying waste their temples uttered by Roman Castevet. Not seeing the baby, we have no chance to judge for ourselves. The only thing that final scene tells us is the strength of the Castevets' belief.

This makes for what was, in 1968, a different kind of horror film. This is not a film about the supernatural, although it certainly borrows elements from the Gothic traditions of Hammer horror in its evocation of witches and demons; and even included a cameo from the film's producer, William Castle, known for his low-grade B-movie horrors in the old histrionic style. What this film represented was 'a passing of the torch from the Old Horror to the New' (Zinoman, 2011: 17). Set in the modern idiom, in twentieth-century New York, those old Gothic concepts are removed from their traditional settings of castles, mystical forests and weird landscapes. In doing this, Polanski was able to use the banality of the urban setting to project a more insidious horror. The terror from the film does not arise from the revelation that Satan is loose upon the world. It is something much more sinister. It is a story of overreaching ambition, and the thirst for power. It is the desire of human beings to influence the world around them and to change it for their own ends and to achieve it no matter what price other people may pay, what suffering is caused them. Not being able to blame evil on an outside agency, but realising that it comes from people themselves, makes for a truly effective horror.

FOOTNOTES

1. For an account of the conscious tendency of the Hammer production teams to create the films almost as if on a treadmill with the re-use of sets, see Hutchings, 1993: 10-11.
2. See Martin Shaw's account of making the film and his take on the extent of Polanski's autocratic work practice, in Parker, 1993: 182.
3. Julia Ain-Krupa has defended the film, finding that the negative response to it arises from a failure to recognise the work as 'a tribute to Polanski's Polish-Jewish roots' (2010: 59). See also Mazierska, 2007: 169-70.
4. For a detailed technical explanation of how this was achieved using camera and lens effects, see Caputo, 2012: 121-3.
5. The skill of Polanski's direction in prompting a particular response from an audience, especially in *Rosemary's Baby*, is described in an anecdote by Bill Fraker in Schaefer and Salvato, 2013: 138-9.

CHAPTER 2: VIOLENCE IN *MACBETH* – 'STEEPED IN BLOOD ...'

In *Rosemary's Baby*, we are invited to empathise with Rosemary, to share her growing terror. This was effective since the horror was generated in that film by the familiarity and banality of the urban environment that foregrounded the very animalistic desires of the people who inhabited it. In exploring another story of the primal desires of human ambition, the drive to have and wield power, a very different setting allowed for this idea to be explored on a much more visceral level. Shakespeare's *Macbeth* offered Polanski much more scope for a realisation of the evil inherent in the human condition in its setting of eleventh-century Scotland and the story of feuding, warlike tribes where power and authority is maintained – and conserved – through sustained violent struggle. Polanski was able to express the idea of the underlying desire for power in the human condition that leads to evil in *Macbeth* by making extensive use of a recognised horror trope allowed by the more primitive setting – blood and gore.

Such an innovation was not without its controversies, many of which distracted initially from Polanski's achievements. Namely, that the sight of blood and gory effects were considered to be a substitute for subtlety and merely present to provide an unhealthy stimulus for the gratification of the coarser natures of the audience. This had been a common complaint against the horror genre, epitomised by the critical reaction to *The Curse of Frankenstein* in 1957, that particular Hammer horror film being noted for its so-called 'Kensington gore', the bright red blood oozing from various supernatural eviscerations. The 1960s had seen a gradual rise in a new form of horror film, one that exploited such visceral visions to the full. Films from Mario Bava's *Black Sunday* (1960) to George A. Romero's *Night of the Living Dead* (1968) were introducing a new type of horror, one that made full use of grisly effects.

Critical responses to the presence of violence in horror films such as these sometimes dismissed its presence as unaesthetic. The initial responses to *The Curse of Frankenstein* contained some criticism of its perceived 'atrocities', such as dismembered limbs and eye evisceration (Harmes, 2015: 25). Even while recognising the innovations made to the genre in *Black Sunday,* critics could not resist chastising Bava for 'unadulterated horror'.[1] Excessive violence and bloodletting in such films was, for some reviewers and critics, symptomatic of a directorial adherence to 'cheap thrills', to the cultivation of a sensational 'quick fix', as opposed to a focus on creating a work of artistic merit. For such critics as these, explicit gore in horror tended to be associated with the genre's status as a staple of popular culture, as part of its accordance with 'lowbrow' cultural interests (see Cherry, 2009: 12).

Macbeth, on its release, met with a similar reaction and such responses epitomise common critical approaches to the film both on its release and the subsequent complaints that were levelled against it – namely that it was 'unShakespearean'. The (lowbrow) violence in the film was seen to contrast badly with the (highbrow) Shakespeare original. Blood and gore was seen as an inartistic imposition on Shakespeare's play and an unnecessary, attention-seeking imposition at that. *Newsweek* critic Paul Zimmerman complained that: 'All that is good here seems but a pretext for close-ups of knives drawing geysers of blood from the flesh of men, women and children. No chance to revel in gore is passed up' (1972: 94).

There is no denying that violence and bloodshed are certainly prevalent in the film, which was so notable for its gore that it was given an 'X' rating on its release in Britain and an 'R' rating in America. The reaction of the early critics is understandable since they were invariably comparing the film to more restrained previous theatrical and cinematic productions. That the play, even when first produced would still, as a matter of course, have been subject to censorship, led to many disparaging comparisons between Shakespeare's artistic restraint in his depiction of violent subject matter and what was seen as Polanski's gratuitous use of blood.

The problems with such comparisons of Polanski's film with Shakespearean artistry were compounded by a particular innovation made by him to Shakespeare's play – the youth of the protagonists. Not only was such an idea considered 'unShakespearean', the use of such young performers was interpreted as an attempt to render the violence in the film more palatable, more appealing.

That the actors playing the lead roles should be young had been one of the first decisions Polanski had made about the film. Such a choice was not a fanciful one; that it had a sound, scholarly basis is seen in the response of one of the greatest theatre critics of the age. Polanski told his collaborator, Kenneth Tynan, that he wanted the Macbeths 'to be young, in their twenties' (Parker, 1993: 177) which went against the grain of many theatrical productions of the play that were largely 'vehicles for aged Hamlets and pensioned Ophelias' (Freud, 1971: 32). It was this proposed change of presenting the Macbeths as young, played by Jon Finch and Francesca Annis, then both in their twenties, that intrigued Tynan and was instrumental in his decision to agree to work on the screenplay (Parker, 1993: 177).

This was no mean feat for Polanski. Himself a maverick, the front man for a new avant-garde and not above courting controversy, Tynan had already tried to work with Polanski to film short pieces for his erotic revue *Oh! Calcutta* in 1969, a project that failed due to Polanski's expensive technical requirements. The revue was a part of Tynan's long association with the British theatre. When Polanski knew him, Tynan was Literary Manager at the National Theatre but he had already had some experience of writing for film, having been a script editor and co-writer at London's Ealing Studios. Tynan's work was always flavoured with his own flamboyant personality; but behind the archness and camp was intellectual rigour and an encyclopaedic knowledge of English literature. He was a man with a love of the old but a grasp of the new. This, and his theatrical credentials, made him a perfect collaborator for Polanski.

Being open to new ideas, and as a theatre critic, Tynan had championed a new type of play that had emerged in the 1950s, the so-called 'Angry Young Man' works, such as John Osborne's *Look Back In Anger* (1956), a play that exemplified the disaffection of contemporary life presented with a brutal and startling realism. It was also a play that was relentlessly associated with youth.[2] This meant that, more than anyone, Tynan understood the reasons behind Polanski's preoccupation with the idea. Presenting the Macbeths as young was a decision that would cause some irritation amongst the reviewers, but Polanski's reasoning was sound. It made Macbeth's ambition more plausible. He would become not a world-weary adult, but a vibrant, driven young man.

Tynan knew, too, that other possibilities for the depiction of evil in the play could be opened up by having the Macbeths portrayed as youthful. Young people in the dramas of the 1960s are not so unimpeachable as their adult counterparts and *Macbeth* is no exception. The youth and good looks of these protagonists and their willingness to commit violent deeds would give such acts a seductive allure. An older couple, childless, thwarted throughout their lives by their perceived lack of achievement lends focus in the play to the more ruminative qualities of Shakespeare's character. He is one who broods on possibilities, who has always brooded on such things and hesitates before acts of violence; but a younger man, eager to succeed, who has spent most of his military career in battle fighting to win, might more readily achieve his ambitions by bloodier means and not be troubled by moral vacillation.

Naturally, the critics disagreed, illustrating one common problem with the early responses to the film – that the blood and violence portrayed was a lowbrow imposition on what was considered essentially a misreading of Shakespeare's lead characters; but, there are two other significant factors that led to the initial response to the violence as being aesthetically inappropriate. Responses to the 'geysers of blood' shown in *Macbeth* have also been coloured by a consideration of the real-life horrors that Polanski experienced.[3]

Many of the early critical responses to the film associated the revelling 'in gore' in part to Polanski's traumatised childhood, as a witness to Hitler's invasion of Poland in 1939. He lived in one of the first ghettos in the city and his father was one of the many Jews taken from such places to a concentration camp; his mother died in Auschwitz. Polanski escaped in 1943 and was sheltered by a Catholic family. During this traumatic period, he witnessed and experienced many acts of motiveless cruelty: the shooting of a woman in the back at point blank range; running from a group of German soldiers who shot at him for fun.[4]

These comparisons are not as potent as one other incident that has encouraged autobiographical readings of the film and that, for some critics, was instrumental in Polanski's choice of the play and the presentation of its horrors. This was the murder of his wife Sharon Tate and their unborn child by cult leader Charles Manson and his followers in August 1969. Believing in an oncoming apocalypse which he called 'Helter Skelter' after a Beatles song of the same name, Manson had acquired a bevy of mainly female followers known as 'the family'. They were in thrall to him, subdued by his psychopathic charm and utterly subservient. Their worship of him reached an horrific peak on 8 August 1969 when Manson declared that the apocalypse was imminent and instructed them to kill the inhabitants of Polanski's rented home on Cielo Drive in Beverly Hills, including Sharon Tate and the couple's friends. Four of his followers committed the most brutal murders, including the multiple stabbing of the pregnant Tate.[5]

In the initial Hollywood newspaper reports of the incident, these real-life murders were conflated with Polanski's films and reported as if they were a scene from something he had directed himself. The killings were spoken of as a scene from a horror film exploring 'the dark and melancholy corners of the human character' (q. Polanski, 1984: 271) – the kind of film for which Polanski was becoming known. A horror-style 'back story' was created by journalists to explain how the killings came about, namely, that they were the outcome of 'black magic', 'rites', 'ritual' and 'witchcraft'. *Time* magazine echoed the Hollywood response to the killings by describing Polanski's artistic motivation as deriving from his feeling 'most at home dealing with black magic' and having an 'affection for the supernatural' (q. Polanski, 1984: 297). It sometimes reads as if the reporters had been watching *Black Sunday* and were imagining they had witnessed the grisly dénouement of a horror film.

Such was this association of Polanski's work and the real-life Manson murders that, inevitably, when Polanski chose to start making *Macbeth* the following year, his motivation was seen as less to do with the simple desire to make a Shakespeare film and more to do with a response to the murders.[6] This assumption led to the early response to the film not as a horror film *per se*, but as a film that was inspired by horror. Even though Polanski himself said that he chose that time to make a Shakespeare film 'because I thought that Shakespeare, at least, would preserve my motives from suspicion' (1984: 297), the first reviews of the film presented the Manson murders as instrumental in Polanski's choice of the play. The violence in the film was not thought to be derived from Shakespeare's work at all, but rather reflecting Polanski's own response to the incident, the horror of the film treated as a cathartic expression of Polanski's own grief: 'It is impossible to watch certain scenes,' noted Roger Ebert, 'without thinking of the Charles Manson case.' He made the connection, as did many others, with Macduff's line 'From my mother's womb untimely ripp'd' (5.7.45-6) and the murder of Tate (2009: 448). Pauline Kael drew parallels between the murder of Lady Macduff in the film and the Manson murders. The equation of the two was so powerful that, even as late as 1996, she was able to recall how the scene had made her feel physically ill (Brantley, 1996: 31).

This early assumption that the violence in the film was influenced by, and made as a response to events in Polanski's own life is not quite so prevalent in more recent criticism of the film as will become apparent: and it does show that while an awareness of the real-life horrors may have affected Polanski's own response to Shakespeare's play, it should not be allowed to overpower a reading of the film to its detriment. It is necessary to look past aspects of Polanski's biography and see the film in the light of his skills as a director of horror, as a work by the creator of *Rosemary's Baby*. In doing so, it can be seen that there are perfectly sound artistic reasons for the amount of bloodshed in *Macbeth*.

Having said that, even in this context, it could be argued that the bloodletting in *Macbeth* is a little excessive. Audiences that had seen *Rosemary's Baby* would have noticed it to be remarkably bloodless and it is adapted from a source that is itself not over-laden with gore. Similarly, in Shakespeare's *Macbeth* some of the violence is offstage, such as the murder of Duncan (played by Nicholas Selby). It is not *necessarily* a spectacularly violent play. In the film, however, 'whereas Shakespeare tells of gore, Polanski pours it' (Deats, 1986: 87). At every opportunity film expresses what stage cannot necessarily achieve, allowing for the visual rendition of violence and its consequences. If it is offstage in the play, in the film, it is in front of us. The Thane of Cawdor (Vic Abbott), when his treachery is revealed, is first shown shackled on a board by chains and dragged behind a horse. His death, only reported in the text, is shown in full by Polanski. He is seen, still chained, in the centre of the castle courtyard, and led up a flight of steps. He jumps, apparently willingly, off the wall and we hear and see the jerk of the chains as he meets his death.

When it is in front of us, it cannot be avoided: 'Polanski sears our eyes with violence' (Kliman, 2004: 192). Not just the acts themselves but their consequences. There are a number of corpses that are seen in the film, and that remain in view, a number not possible in the smaller theatrical performance space. In this film, corpses are not generally disposed of, but are left lying around in full view. After the credits, we see a battlefield littered with bodies that remain in view throughout the wide shots used during the scene. The Thane of Cawdor is left in full view, swinging on his chains, like the prisoners hanging in rows behind Macbeth when we first see him. Seyton's corpse is on view at the end when the thanes desert Macbeth. Even the effect of self-inflicted violence is shown. When Lady Macbeth dies, her disjointed, misshapen body is left where it falls, seen by the absconding thanes and inspected by Macduff as he enters the castle. No one corpse is disposed of, not even royalty. Duncan's body is always in view – crumpled on the floor of the bedroom, then laid out on the bed and, finally, dressed for the funeral procession.

Polanski exploits any reference to blood in the play to the full, using the film medium for a graphic representation not necessarily possible on stage. From the very beginning, this is a film as 'blood-boltered' (4.1.138) as Banquo's ghost. When the mist clears after the opening credits, we see a man lying on a beach who is pounded to death by a mace with 'two or three sickening whacks' (Rothwell, 2004: 148) that leave a dark, spreading stain on his back. Polanski takes literally Shakespeare's line 'What bloody man is that?' (1.2.1) by showing the first story of Macbeth's victories as told by a soldier (Frank Wylie) whose eye is closed from the battering he has received and whose face is covered in blood. There is even sardonic laughter at the mention of a disembowelling, Macdonwald being 'unseamed ... from the nave to the chops' (1.2.22). The bloody consequences of battle are here depicted with unflinching realism.

Even the presentation of such fighting in the film shows Polanski exploiting the medium to the full, charging the fight scenes with an indecorous brutality at every opportunity. The final encounter between Macbeth and Macduff is not presented as a clash of noblemen, all ringing swords and gleaming shields; but savage, blunt and brutal and played out in front of a large cast of supporting actors as Malcolm's army. The encounter is not at all chivalrous, but, rather a maelstrom of animal-like grunts, wet thumps of battered flesh, thuds and dings of armour. Weaponry is whatever is to hand – swords, axes, logs, fists, ending with Macbeth speared and decapitated, his trunk juddering down the steps, while 'blood gushes from the wound' of his severed neck (Rothwell, 1973: 75).

Such sights show that this is a film in which blood wells around wounds, sprays and spatters from daggers, and swords, hands are smeared and coated with it. Shakespeare's metaphorical quantities in the text are supported by the visual realisation in the film. Duncan's bloodied body illustrates Lady Macbeth's somnambulistic 'Who would have thought the old man to have had so much blood in him' (5.1.36-8). The sight of the blood being washed away with water from a well, running along the castle stones is a striking visual realisation of Macbeth's own horror that the amount of blood on his hands cannot be cleaned even by an ocean of water – 'this my hand will rather / The multitudinous seas incarnadine / Making the green one red' (2.2.60-2).

All that these aspects of the violence in the film have in common is that they are generally literal realisations of Shakespeare's imagery. Russell Jackson notes that any responses to filmed Shakespeare have always been coloured by this 'anxiety about the visualised image usurping the spoken word's legitimate function' (2007: 25). The sight of Macbeth saying the lines and then a shot of the water running red in the gutters of the castle caused uneasiness amongst the early reviewers who thought such 'geysers of blood' were gratuitously foisted onto Shakespeare's text, and undermined its poetry.

What Polanski has done, however, is expand upon the play's themes of savagery and brutality by adding visual metaphor to the verbal. In *Macbeth*, violence is present metaphorically as well as physically. Violent deaths are themselves prefigured by violent visual metaphors. Duncan's grooms (played by Bill Drysdale and Roy Jones) are seen performing a dangerous dance after the feast at Macbeth's house, drunkenly leaping barefoot around and over swords. Their death is foreshadowed by Macbeth's first sight of them in their drunken and drugged stupor with the redness of the spilled wine around them standing in for blood. Implicated by Lady Macbeth in the murder of Duncan they are shown, in another scene not in Shakespeare's play, after they are killed by Macbeth, their dismembered corpses providing such a horrible sight that one character in the film faints at its bloodiness.

Not just sights, but sounds underscore the violence. When, towards the end of the film, Macduff (Terence Bayler) is lamenting the murder of 'all my pretty chickens and their dam / At one fell swoop' (4.3.218-9), behind him swords are being sharpened, the grinding of the metal buzzing throughout his words. It serves as a visual representation of Malcolm's inducement to him to allow his grief to be 'the whetstone of your sword' (4.3.228); but the intermittent sound, its intrusive disharmony, serves as an audible reminder of the 'savage' murders and the torment and feelings of revenge that are grinding within Macduff himself.

By 'searing' our eyes in the realisation of Shakespeare's poetic and metaphorical bloodiness with actual brutality, and underscoring it with visual and aural details such as these, Polanski is not detracting from the play. It only takes a slight adjustment in perspective to find the reasons for its inclusion. Such a perspective is to consider it in the context of horror, whereby a whole new meaning to the presentation of the blood and gore in the film can be discerned. In this light, the violence in the film does not appear gratuitous. Instead, it adds depth to the story. There is more going on here than simply the audience's titillation. The depiction of blood-drenched scenes only referred to in the original play are there to create in the viewer a visceral response to the horror before them, the very *raison d'être* of the horror genre. Those early reviewers clearly had that feeling, but they misconstrued it as cheap thrills. They did not realise that those feelings were *meant* to have a 'shock value', that they were signs of Polanski directing the audience's response to the horror just as he had with *Rosemary's Baby*.

An example of this can be seen in the presentation of the murder of Duncan. This is not shown in Shakespeare's play, but here is portrayed in all its bloody glory. It is not merely a visual rendering of the murder, however. Polanski adds suspense to the sequence. This is a familiar horror trope usually described as analogous to a 'rollercoaster' after Stephen King's description, identifying the expectation of a violent act from a suspenseful build up. Polanski shows Macbeth enter the chamber and, framed in the doorway, linger over the bed of the sleeping king. He slowly toys with his intended victim, hesitating whether to kill him, pushing back the king's nightshirt and exposing his chest. When Duncan stirs and recognises who is standing over him, dagger in hand, Macbeth strikes suddenly and violently, stabbing him eight or nine times in the chest. It does not end there. When the groaning Duncan slides off the bed, Macbeth lunges forward and administers one final, fatal blow, pushing the dagger directly into Duncan's throat.

The scene has a powerful build up and dénouement. It also shows Polanski as a master of his craft. Whereas the horror in *Rosemary's Baby* relied for its thrills on presenting Rosemary's possibly distorted view of the world, and inviting us to empathise with her growing terror without actually showing anything especially gruesome, *Macbeth* gains its tingle by appealing to the very basic and primitive instincts in human nature as we watch Duncan's murder in action. Polanski *intends* it to be animalistic. The violence is there deliberately as an expression of the animal aspect beneath the civilised exterior.

This is in keeping with the larger world of the film, where Polanski expresses the underlying savagery of this human society by the literal presentation of animals as creatures who are subject to, and inflict, violence. Chickens squawk and flap as they are taken to be slaughtered, pigs squeal and wriggle to get away from the same fate. Hawks, animals that are tamed to hunt on our behalf provide a powerful visual metaphor in the film for the violent actions of the humans. A hawk is seen in shot before Banquo leaves the castle after Macbeth's coronation, a foretelling of his own fate to be hunted and killed. His ghost at the banquet lunges toward Macbeth with a hawk on his arm, making explicit the connection between the hunter and the hunted. Before the murder of Lady Macduff and her son, attention is drawn to two birds by one of the thugs (Ian Hogg), sitting, hooded on their perch. Here, again, a foretelling of the fate of Macduff's family.

Even Macbeth has a parallel in an animal. One of the film's most notorious scenes shows the practice of bear baiting. For some critics this was a rather clumsy realisation of one of Shakespeare's most powerful metaphors in the play, an example of the 'occasional over-deliberate enactment of imagery' that Jackson cites (2007: 25). When, at the end of the play, Macbeth feels trapped, he likens himself to a chained bear set upon by dogs: 'They have tied me to a stake. I cannot fly / But, bearlike, I must fight the course' (5.7.1-2). In the film, after watching bear baiting in the castle, Macbeth later sees the ring on the post by which the bear had been chained and this prompts him to speak those lines. The connection between Macbeth and the bear is further underlined when he is seen later in the film wearing a cloak of animal fur that may well be made from the pelt of the slaughtered bear, whose corpse we see dragged out of sight leaving a trail of blood in its wake.

For a few commentators this presentation of Shakespeare's language was symptomatic of Polanski's tendency to make literal the metaphorical and thus, somehow, rob it of its power. However, it can be argued equally that Polanski has not undermined the metaphor, but, rather, has added a new layer. The explicit comparisons made between the bear and Macbeth underscore the animal vitality that has driven him to murder Duncan: and there is a further layer to the image. The bear-baiting scene in the film frames the murder of Banquo. Deats noted that the line 'Here's our chief guest' (3.1.11) is directed, not at Banquo as it is in the play, but at the bear, 'thereby linking the beast with the other "guest" selected by Macbeth for murder' (1986: 88). In Polanski's film while Macbeth may feel as if he is the chained bear fighting for his life, in reality he is one of the dogs that savagely kill.

In using the animals this way, Polanski was underscoring the penchant for blood that underlies the civilised exterior; and in showing the murder of Duncan in full he was illustrating, and at the same time appealing to, that very animalistic part of humanity that gives any horror film its intrinsic thrill. This does not mean that he was in any way detracting from his Shakespearean source. Indeed as far as Shakespeare is concerned, much recent criticism has defended Polanski's use of violence as being true to Shakespeare's play (see Deats, 1986: 92n3). Critics such as Per Serritslev Petersen argue that, 'For the record: Polanski did not put the "bloody business", the gory violence in Macbeth, for it was already there, in Shakespeare's play' (1994: 48). Some commentators thought that to focus on the violence and bloodshed in the film was a misinterpretation of both the film and its source. Jack J. Jorgens considered that any violence 'is not the central focus of the film any more than it is the central focus of Shakespeare's play' (1977: 174). Others have noted that the presence of violence and blood in the film is not as endemic as it might first appear. Deats remarked that 'except for the savage hacking of the opening scene, the screen does not bleed red' until after the murder of Duncan (1986: 87).

It is in this light that another notorious scene should be regarded: the murder of Lady Macduff and her son. It was this that caused Pauline Kael such uneasiness in her equation of the murder of a mother and a child with the Manson killings. There is, however, very little violence enacted on the two on screen. The scene begins in domestic bliss, children playing in the castle courtyard. It then moves indoors where Lady Macduff (Diane Fletcher) has been bathing her son (Mark Dightam). The child's nakedness is symbolic of his innocence and vulnerability. After a witty exchange between the two, women's throaty screams are heard. The door opens and three men appear, clearly bent on violence and destruction; but the violence inflicted on Lady Macduff and her son is not at all bloody. It is, in fact, rather restrained. The child is stabbed once in the back from behind and his is the only blood actually seen in the room. What happens to Lady Macduff is implied, rather than shown. She escapes her assailant and runs away. She is then confronted with one woman being restrained and raped and, in running from that, encounters the bloodied corpses of her two other children, lying on sackcloth and straw.

The presentation of this scene provides the clues for the reading of the violence and blood in the play. It is not, as Bernice W. Kliman proposed, what we see – but what we do *not* see. Although she admitted that 'Polanski sears our eyes with violence' in the film, that he takes advantage of the film medium 'to depict it in graphic detail' (2004: 192), she also noted that at the same time 'the film continually exhibits a curious restraint'. We do not see the grooms being killed by Macbeth, we do not see the bear being killed by the dogs – and though her fate is foreshadowed, we do not actually see what happens to Lady Macduff. We are 'barely aware' that her son has been killed, since there is only a small rill of blood from the wound rather than the pulsing gouts of Polanski's special formula blood elsewhere.

Fig. 4. The remarkably bloodless killing of Lady Macduff's son.

This restraint acts, for Kliman, to play on the expectations of the audience and hold a mirror up to them. When we see a scene played out like the murder of Lady Macduff and we do not see it in full, we fill in the unshown violence with our own minds. This, said Kliman, is Polanski asking the question 'Aren't you quite able to imagine what I hint at?' We, as the audience are complicit in such violence because 'don't we *want* Macbeth to get on with Duncan's murder?' This reading is, for her, in accordance with Shakespeare's play, a work which 'leads us to anticipate violence' (2004: 193). This is a point toward Kliman's larger thesis, that Polanski's film is not about the tragedy of one individual, but the tragedy of the society he inhabits. Setting the film in the feudal

Scotland of Raphael Holinshed's *Chronicles*, the source for the play, a country on the verge of forming the social impositions necessary to contain tribal violence (2004: 192), enabled Polanski to depict the 'tragic figure' in the play as 'society itself' (2004: 191). In watching the events of the film unfold, the audience is also watching a society that is a mirror of its own, 'rather than a misanthropic diatribe' (2004: 192). Polanski mines the feudal past to pass comment on our supposedly civilised present.

This is to read the play in terms of its Shakespearean source material, and to reflect on the film as using Shakespeare as a model for social commentary. Such a reading allows for the incorporation of the source material and can be extended into a reading of the film as a horror. To see it in this way, the scene above gains in power. The restraint that Kliman reveals is the ability of Polanski to use a common horror convention to make the scene of the killing of the Macduffs seem *even more horrific*. In horror, the build up of the anticipation to an event, the nervous fear of its outcome provides the terror, the 'finest emotion', according to King (1981: 22). It is the moment of the visceral thrill, the suspense that gives a horror film its power. Once we have seen the monster in the film, or the murder, or the ghost, we then experience feelings of horror, which are mingled with some relief – it could have been worse, it could have been me (King, 1981: 116-7). By not showing what *actually* happens to Lady Macduff, Polanski stretches the terror. Because we do not see what happens to her, we never have that moment of relief, that near-reassurance that 'what's done is done' (3.2.13).

Knowing this, the rest of the violence in the film can be seen in this light. Beyond the physical presence of the blood, which everyone expects to see in a horror film anyway, is the ability of Polanski to sustain these feelings of terror. That is why, at crucial moments, the outcome is left to our imagination. We see the Thane of Cawdor jump, but we do not see him hang. The sound of the chains tightening is enough to make a viewer wince. We see Macbeth draw a sword on the accused grooms, hear the metallic hiss as it is unsheathed, and see its blade glinting in the close-up: but we do not see what he does. We hear the sounds of the bear-baiting, the barking and the growling, but we do not see the actual fight. We know what is happening, however, because we can see Lady Macbeth's reaction to it. She is at once fascinated and appalled by what she sees, unable to take her eyes off the spectacle - which, given her response, in our imaginations we see as gruesome. The suspense is, quite literally dreadful – as in, filling the viewer with a feeling of dread. After all, at any point, the camera may turn and we may see the bear baiting. The fact that we do not, sustains the agony of the terror, and not the relief of the outcome.

Of such stuff is classic horror made – the sustained terror, the fear of the unknown. In this way, Polanski can use these conventions of horror to make fresh his familiar Jacobean source, by adding suspense and terror to a well-known story. The film is peppered with even minor moments of uncertainty. Duncan waking gives the audience a momentary flutter that Macbeth might fail, might realise Lady Macbeth's fear that 'The attempt and not the deed / Confounds us' (2.2.11-12). In the final fight between Macbeth and Macduff, Macbeth nearly wins, his sword pushed against Macduff's chin, as the latter lies unarmed. There is the feeling that, perhaps, as she runs, Lady Macduff will get away. The cumulative effect of such moments is to induce in the watching audience the visceral jolt of anticipation so integral to the horror film.

Macbeth, therefore, can be seen as a horror film and not just because of the sensational amount of violence and gore, but because it shows that Polanski understands what it is that *makes* a horror. This is recognisably the work of the director of *Rosemary's Baby*. In that film, Polanski demonstrated the ability to carry the audience along with a subjective viewpoint to the finale where we empathise so strongly, we feel what Rosemary feels so much, that we begin to imagine we are seeing what she is seeing, a demon in the cradle. Similarly, in his presentation of the violence in *Macbeth*, Polanski is able to carry the viewer along with the *feeling* of the film, to allow the watching audience to experience the terror for themselves. It is recognisable as a horror film – as one that provides a visceral thrill, not in the visual representation of violence, but in the anticipation of it.

FOOTNOTES

1. Eugene Archer, 'Horrors!: Black Sunday, from Italy, Has Premiere', *The New York Times*, 9.3.61.

2. See Tynan's own review concerning the appeal of the play to the young in *The Observer*, 13.5.56.

3. For the tendency of critics to read Polanski's *oeuvre* autobiographically, see Mazierska, 2007: 7-23. Polanski himself has complained of this inclination on the part of the press, telling the reviewer Jerry Oster 'critics don't review the film, they review me' (*New York Sunday News*, 27.6.76).

4.   See *Roman*, 1984: 13-35 for Polanski's own account of life in the ghetto and after his escape.
     For the anecdote about German troops using him for target practice, see Sandford, 2007:
     33-4.

5.   For Polanski's own account of the murders, see Polanski, 1984: 267-83. A full account of the
     incident is in Bugliosi, 1974.

6.   Polanski has himself made very few explicit comparisons between his own experiences and
     whether or not they have been realised in the film. There are only two reports of him doing
     so, both involving the scene of the murder of Lady Macduff and her children. One is that his
     real-life experience of an SS Officer searching the family room in the Warsaw ghetto inspired
     the casual vandalism of Macbeth's thugs in the scene (1984: 291). He also reportedly told
     Kenneth Tynan, who expressed qualms about the amount of bloodshed, 'You didn't see my
     house last summer. I know about bleeding'; see Parker, 1993: 178.

CHAPTER 3: THE PRESENTATION OF THE SUPERNATURAL – 'STRANGE THINGS I HAVE IN HEAD'

Fig. 5. 'Dark night strangles the travelling lamp' – the twilight unease of the play.

That violence can engender a physical response in the audience is exploited by Polanski. It provides one of the key ingredients that make the film a horror, namely the *feel* of it, the emotional response it provokes; but it is not just the bloodshed in Polanski's film that provides this. He creates an atmosphere of nervous unease. After Macbeth's coronation and during the preparations for celebratory feastings, Banquo (Martin Shaw) rides out with his son, Fleance (Keith Chegwin), unknowingly to their doom. As they ride, Banquo speaks lines transferred from Ross: 'By the clock 'tis day / And yet dark night strangles the travelling lamp' (2.4.6-7). Banquo's murder, along with much of the brutality that happens in *Macbeth* occurs in this shadowland between night and day. As with Shakespeare's play, such a setting invokes a feeling in the audience of another world, of a symbolic twilight space between life and death. It creates a sense of unease, along with other evocations of the esoteric in the film – the muted lights, the red sunsets and dawns, the number of times a cock crows, even a Porter (Sydney Bromley) who talks of opening the gates of hell ('Who's there in the name of Beelzebub?': 2.3.3). Such invocations of a mystical netherworld create a queasiness of anticipation, a prickle of impending doom, the very *feel* of a horror.

Creating an expectation that something horrible is about to happen is what a horror film is all about. The visual and aural effects described above make for a creepy atmosphere that is enhanced by Shakespeare's language. Take, for example, the words of Lennox (Andrew Laurence), who arrives at Inverness castle with Macduff to wake Duncan. He adds to the atmosphere of dread surrounding the impending discovery of the king's body when he reports to Macbeth that 'The night has been unruly', expressing himself in that staple of superstition, the hearsay account: 'as they say / lamentings heard in the air / Strange screams of death … / Some say the earth / was feverous, and did shake' (2.3.55-62).

Fig. 6. Lightning strikes the castle.

Like Banquo's speech which was originally Ross' superstitious response to the death of Duncan, Lennox's speech is one of many Gothic markers in the film that lure the viewer into thinking that the otherworldly has a hand in events. Lennox is right about one thing – that the night of Duncan's murder was 'unruly'. There has clearly been a storm – it's arrival is heralded by the rumble of thunder and the subsequent downpour that accompanies Duncan's arrival at the castle. This leads to scenes preceding the murder of the king that are riven with familiar visual Gothic portents. In a scene straight out of the 1931 *Frankenstein*, a bright fork of lightning streaks from the sky towards the old castle; a strong gust of wind suddenly blows open the shutters of a window at the feast and the lamps gutter and are extinguished; the horses in the stables whinny and come crashing through the doors, galloping toward the camera, manes flying in the lashing rain. It is textbook Gothic horror, a night full of omens and portents that we are encouraged to read as having a supernatural origin by Lennox's description. It makes the impending murder of Duncan seem to be the result of demonic influence playing as it does on the cinematic vocabulary of horror. Even the door to the king's chamber creaks ominously when Macbeth closes it.[1]

However, it is worth looking beyond these and recalling what is actually *seen* in the film. Such sights as shutters and doors smashing open may have a much more mundane explanation. Inverness castle shows signs of ongoing restoration – at the top of the stairs is 'a rail of raw wood' that suggests 'recent repairs' (Kliman, 2004: 195). If the building is in need of shoring up, then it is no wonder the door to Duncan's chamber creaks or that the shutter flies open. It takes Banquo two attempts to close it. The wooden stable doors are held together only by a chain that would be easily broken by a startled horse.

The fact that we disregard these aspects and think something supernatural is about to happen is because Polanski has very cleverly used the traditions of the Gothic horror film to raise such an expectation. Even though, as we shall see, the film is punctuated by the sight of alternative truths to these signs of the supernatural we are led by his cinematic sleight-of-hand at this stage to think that this is a film about the supernatural, that there is a numinous force controlling the affairs of the humans. This is an extension of the conceit used in *Rosemary's Baby*, here expressed in Lennox's speech – we think something supernatural is happening because we are told and shown that is so. When, in fact, all we really have is the insistence of Lennox's *belief* in the supernatural; and a rather clever play on Polanski's part of our concessions to those beliefs in the creation of an atmosphere of dreadful suspense.

There is a further dimension to this. Throughout the film, the main reason we think that this is a film about the supernatural is not solely the presence of these Gothic portents. It is because, as with Shakespeare's play, we are invited to share Macbeth's thoughts, in particular, his belief that he is subject to these otherworldly influences. Through a subjective engagement with Macbeth, we follow his belief that he is charged by supernatural forces to act as he does. In such a subjective involvement with Macbeth's interpretation of events as having a supernatural origin, we are at the same time given reminders that they do not. There are, as will be shown throughout this chapter, markers throughout the film that draw our attention to what is happening outside of Macbeth's interpretation. We see that, despite what he believes, the women do not dress or behave like witches, that they do not vanish 'into the air' (1.3.81) but instead disappear into an underground cave. We share his vision of Banquo's ghost but also hear his wife and the court say they have not seen any such thing. We share Macbeth's experiences of the prophecies that he thinks will save him, but know there is no coven of supernatural fiends and demonic spirits that he believes have foreseen his fate.

This effect, this lack of any objective evidence of the supernatural in the film means that Polanski was able to reveal the far more insidious horror that he had also shown in *Rosemary's Baby* – an exploration of the evil that is perpetrated by humans in their ambitions and desire for power.

*

To explore the presentation of the supernatural in this way would also answer the concerns of some critics for whom such elements in Shakespeare's play – the witches, the ghost and the prophecies – were not fully realised by Polanski. This was in some ways due to that hoary old argument presented against horror, namely its low cultural status. When these supernatural elements are transferred to a Shakespeare film they can sometimes be seen by critics in a rather negative light, as part of a tradition of the mass (lowbrow) appeal of modern cinematic horror superimposed upon (highbrow) Shakespeare.

Thus, some Shakespeare critics find Polanski's handling of the supernatural in the film an uneasy mix of the Gothic horror demanded by a mass cinema audience and the subtle nuances of the horrific in Shakespeare's text. Storms and portents, for these critics, were incompatible with Shakespeare's poetry. For Neil Forsyth, Polanski appeared to be torn between the expectations of an audience becoming used to the new Hollywood cinematic realism in horror, and the presentation of Shakespeare's rich verbal imagery that expresses the supernatural aspects of the play. Forsyth considered that aspects such as the realisation of the witches in the film were 'confusing' because Polanski 'was working within the naturalistic conventions of Hollywood, which left him rather lost when it came to the supernatural bits'. For him, the film:

> ...lacks any context, inherited or invented, within which to represent the sheer *strangeness* of the play. He sets the film in a pre-Christian Scotland given over to a demonic cult, yet visually his witches are no 'secret black and midnight hags' [4.1.62]. Though they are certainly not attractive, Polanski chooses to present these ambivalent creatures as rural women, not devilish spirits: they keep goats, they live in daylight... (2007: 288-9; my emphasis)

Here, for Forsyth, there is an inherent wrongness in this earthy realism of the women since they are characters that would be expected to form a part of the queasy 'strangeness' of the atmosphere. This is the second, repeated accusation against the film – that it is 'unShakespearean'. Forsyth's interpretation stems from a literal reading of Shakespeare's work based upon an assumption that the supernatural occurrences in the play are 'real', that the weird sisters have the ability to use occult powers to affect the outcome of events, to influence people. That, in Shakespeare, there really are witches. This leads to an expectation on Forsyth's part, that the representation of the women in the film should reflect their diabolical potential.

'... THIS BLASTED HEATH'

To understand why Polanski presents the weird woman in the way that he does, it is necessary to look, firstly, at the context in which he places them. To do this would lay the foundations for an understanding of the larger role of the presentation of the supernatural within the film and defend it against the charges laid out above. That first sight of the three women occurs on Polanski's version of Shakespeare's 'blasted heath' (1.3.77), outdoors on a vast landscape of sea and sky. This opening shot is an indication that, despite Forsyth's reservations, the film has a definite context. Very little happens in the film within a completely closed space. From the very outset, the action in *Macbeth* is set largely outdoors – battles, the hanging of prisoners, even the first encounter of Macbeth and Banquo and the women. So ubiquitous is the fresh air of Snowdonia that stood in for Scotland, that even in scenes taking place within walls, they also still happen outdoors, since they occur under roofless castle courtyards. Domestic scenes are played out underneath the sky – Lady Macbeth reads her husband's letter whereby he announces his encounter with the women in the courtyard of her castle, outlined by the reddish glow of the sun. Such courtyards are the centre of activity in the film, more so than the indoors, overrun with animals and with people attending to the business of the households – as Lady Macduff's children play in the courtyard at Fife, someone is shearing a sheep.

Even when indoors, the outside is always present. We look through windows from the outside to the inside, watching the preparations for Duncan's settling in for the night; and look from the inside to the outside, with Macbeth as he delivers his 'Come, seeling night' (3.2.49) speech. The outdoors is always materially present, even when we are seemingly securely indoors – dust rises from Macbeth's cape as Duncan embraces him, flower petals are scattered on a bed, straw and animals share the beds of soldiers. Having the outdoors always visibly present indoors shows that, in *Macbeth*, the man-made environment does not necessarily represent stability. The imposition on the stone structure of a castle contrasts the implied stability of a domestic environment enacted in those buildings with an unrefined nature. It emphasises how such structures are indelibly linked to the outdoors; that, in the wider order of nature, buildings like castles are temporary impositions upon the landscape; and that, ultimately, nature has primacy over the human built environment.

This is a theme in the film we have encountered before. This idea that nature has primacy hearkens back to Polanski's use of violence in the film whereby its presence is an invocation of the primal desires that lurk beneath the civilised exterior. This is assisted in the setting of the film, which Forsyth rightly identified as being set in a 'Pre-Christian Scotland'. Polanski placed the film in the eleventh century, the same as the source book for the play, Raphael Holinshed's *Chronicles*.[2] By following the play and setting the action in this era, rather than modernising it, Polanski evokes a time when people were dependent on the landscape for their survival and struggled to shape or tame it. The film is full of images of how the environment provides the very raw stuff for living. Rock and stone is hewn and shaped to build castles. Within those castle walls, animals roam freely and their use is emphasised – they are taken away for feasting, they provide entertainment in the form of bear baiting, their wool is spun into thick cloth, such as the blanket that covers Macbeth when he stirs from sleep after the visit to the weird women. Animal hides are crudely stitched to make tents and clothes, such as the tunic worn by Macbeth when he emerges from the tent and the boots that he ties after he has heard that he is promoted to Thane of Cawdor.[3] There is metal cast into swords and maces, metal which also binds Cawdor in chains of punishment and is shaped into the medallion that is Macbeth's reward for valour; and is forged into armour that Macbeth puts on as he prepares to fight Malcolm and his army.

Fig. 7. The opening shot.

Yet, even as there is evidence of this shaping and use of the natural world, the sheer scale of the landscape in the film diminishes those attempts. The film medium allows for the use of the landscape and its vastness to underscore the prevailing idea that nature still has primacy over the human endeavour in a way that stage-based theatrical performances cannot. This is most effectively realised in the opening scene of the film. Here, Polanski eschews all sight of human occupation and focuses on the elemental, the raw stuff of nature. The opening shot alone encompasses water, sand, sky and cloud, before even the women shuffle into view. The first sight is of a beach at sunrise with the red sky reflected in the water below. The eye is filled with this vast landscape of reddened clouds and ribbed, wet sand. Then the sky slowly lightens[1] and the colour changes from a bloody red to a murky blue; but the camera remains still, unmoving. The focus does not shift. The first sound to be heard is not human, but animal – the screech of a gull as it flies across the screen. Even that is in the distance. Not until the bird has flown across the screen from left to right and is out of the picture does something appear in a close up: and then, it is not a person but a stick, fashioned from a tree branch.

The power of this opening shot and its significance has not gone unnoticed by critics. All of them see it as a suggestive prelude of the drama to come, of the path taken by Macbeth on his rise to power. For some, it simply represents the story in a symbolic shorthand. Julia Ain-Krupa describes the opening as 'a desert of flaming red, signifying burning desire, and the flame that burns itself out' (2010: 79). The prevailing view of the symbolic value of this opening shot is largely that of many theatre critics. In the vision of such a bleak, vast landscape, some of them have seen an analogy with the British contemporary theatre, 'the theatrical and critical avant-garde of the sixties'. In particular, 'the hopeless, miserable world of Samuel Beckett and absurdist drama' (Williams, 2004: 148). This is to equate the opening scene of *Macbeth* with the landscape of dramas such as Beckett's *Waiting For Godot* and its static, nonspecific setting, symbolic of an indifferent, unchanging universe. This idea found favour with Per Serritslev Petersen who described the opening scene as a 'cosmic *tabula rasa*'. For him, it is a setting so barren and vast that it is 'unnatural' (1994: 46).

To be fair, this is not a wholly inaccurate reading of Polanski's opening shot. The vastness of the view, the subdued sounds, are bound to make a cinema audience, faced with the view on a gigantic screen, feel lost, even displaced; but it has to be said that, far from being bleak and forbidding, an image of a cold and indifferent universe, the opening shot of the rising sun is not 'unnatural' at all. It is *nothing but* natural, and actually quite beautiful. Its grandeur, the lingering view of the slow sunrise, is pleasing to the eye.

In that respect, nor is it a particularly horror-inspiring landscape. The whole opening scene might be seen as the very antithesis of horror since it does not begin, as does Shakespeare's play, with a very obvious supernatural sequence. There was certainly plenty of scope for Polanski and Tynan to have opened the film with a crack of lightning and a rumble of thunder and the sight of three gibbering old hags. The fact that it does not perhaps explains the perplexity of critics like Forsyth, since all of that is right there in the very stage directions of the play. Instead, what we have are Forsyth's 'rural women' (played by Maisie MacFarquhar, Elsie Taylor and, the youngest, Noelle Rimmington). That they are impoverished countrywomen is a deliberate attempt to incorporate them into the countryside they inhabit, that we see in the opening shot. Although they are seen in close-up, almost obscuring the view of the landscape behind them, this is not to isolate them from their surroundings, but to render them a part of it.[5] The first item seen is a natural object, a stick, rather than a person. It is an object hewn from the landscape, from the greenery in the far distance of the shot. Thus the first object equates the person holding it, the woman, with the environment into which she emerges.

That the women are an integral part of the landscape in which we first see them is also achieved by the diminution of Shakespeare's own language in this first scene. In the play, the stage direction marks the entrance of the three women with thunder and lightning and one of the most famous opening lines in dramatic – and, for that matter, horror – history: 'When shall we three meet again?' (1.1.1). Not so in Polanski's film. There is no storm and it is the best part of two minutes before the women chant 'Fair is foul, and foul is fair.' (1.1.11) Not in unison either, but in an arhythmic, ever-so-slightly discordant way. The well-known opening speech of the witches in the play is here merely an arrangement to meet ('Where the place? / Upon the heath': 1.1.6) while they pack the cart – not a prelude to sinister events.

Fig. 8. The women dig in the sand.

This alone would be enough to render any self-respecting Shakespearean apoplectic; but Polanski goes yet further. He substitutes the words with extended action. The opening of the film is not focused, as in the play, on the women's conversation overheard, but on the ritual they perform – in silence. They mark a circle and then dig a hole in the sand and bury objects within it. There is a hangman's noose, and they then unwrap a dead man's hand. This is perhaps a 'hand of glory', severed from the man who had been hanged. It is most likely that the noose buried with it is his own and the cloth in which the hand is wrapped is a piece of the man's shroud. A dagger is carefully placed in the hand and all is then covered over with the sand.[6] After pouring some blood on the ground and chanting, the women spit east, south and west. They arrange to meet, then walk slowly away, into the distance, the younger woman dragging the cart behind them as they are gradually enshrouded by a mist which they have not conjured, but which has been approaching since the first gleams of the opening shot.

For some critics, having all of this action and few words was going too far, deliberately undermining Shakespeare. John Russell Brown found these actions of the women work 'without building expectation or establishing any ritual gravity' (2005: 140). On the contrary, the scene is deeply, and seriously ritualistic and that lengthy process, enabled by the visual medium of film, arguably enriching Shakespeare's first scene. By subduing the opening speeches of the women, Polanski embeds them in that vast landscape. Their words are not declaimed, or given any focus. They are part of the soundtrack of screeching gulls, distant waves and the sound of the Third Ear Band. It establishes the women as a part of that environment, not separate from it. But it also means that all of the supernatural trappings that are associated with Shakespeare's opening scene are diminished in their importance.

This is also why the women look the way that they do, as 'rural women'. They are, as Forsyth noted, anything but 'black and midnight hags' (4.1.62). As an integral part of the landscape they inhabit their physical appearance underlines this. They are not, as Sara M. Deats pointed out 'awesome Fates or screaming evil furies'. They are 'ordinary, frumpy, old and young women' (1986: 86). Bernice W. Kliman described them as 'desperate peasants' whose 'living arrangements, with sacks and barrows, goats and pails, domesticate them' (2004: 202). Such homely accoutrements shows them to be people who depend upon the landscape for survival in the keeping of animals, and who use the raw materials of nature to build what they need – wood for walking sticks, carts and improvised shelters, animal hides for clothes and cover. Seeing the women in this definitively rural context, part of the landscape and not separate from it, implants in the mind of the audience that these women are real, not supernatural manifestations. They, like their surroundings, have a material presence in the film that cannot be avoided or mistaken for a vision.

The only person who sees in them any illusory qualities is Macbeth himself. When he first encounters them and they announce their prophecies, it is Banquo, not he, who wonders aloud whether they are real: they 'look not like the inhabitants of the earth / And yet are on it' (1.3.41-2). In truth, he asks, 'Are ye fantastical / Or that indeed which outwardly do show?' (1.3.52-4) That they are very real is shown when Macbeth dismounts and follows them, demanding to know more. The women run away, down some steps into an underground cave. What is important here is that, although he witnesses this, Macbeth's response to Banquo's question 'Whither have they vanished?' is to say 'into the air' (1.3.80-1). They quite clearly have not.

Immediately, this is an interesting perspective on Macbeth's character. Why does he tell Banquo that the women disappeared as if they were ghosts – 'what seemed corporal melted, as breath into the wind' (1.3.81-2)? Especially as one of them has lifted her skirts and presumably shown him that she is, indeed, all woman. Perhaps it is because, for him, if Banquo is right and they are spiritual beings, not a gaggle of strange-looking women encountered in the middle of nowhere, their prophecies might come true.

'BE NOT LOST SO POORLY IN YOUR THOUGHTS'

This is our first glimpse of the presentation in the film of two different realities. That which is shown to be Macbeth's and that which we see is otherwise. A group of rural women chanting and someone who believes that such incantations are more than they seem. Whatever his initial motive might be, the important point is that the women are given a supernatural, otherwordly presence because Macbeth *chooses* to interpret them that way. We are encouraged to think that Macbeth believes what he saw as having some occult significance and that it was not the product of any 'insane root / that takes the reason prisoner' (1.3.84-5) in the highlighting of a particular aspect of Macbeth's character, a trait with which Banquo is familiar. When he hears what the witches have to say, he glances over at Macbeth, who does not speak. This prompts Banquo to comment that his friend 'seems rapt withall' (1.3.57). Later, when told that he has been made Thane of Cawdor, Macbeth succumbs to a meditation upon 'supernatural soliciting' that yields a 'horrid image' of murder (1.3.131, 136). So much so, that he does not mount his horse, and it is Banquo who observes with the ease of one who knows his friend well, 'Look how our partner's rapt' (1.3.143) and prompts him with 'we stay upon your leisure' (1.3.149).

Polanski places a special emphasis on this habit of his protagonist, adding additional business to one scene to underscore its importance. Macbeth's tendency to be 'rapt' is not only noticed by Banquo but also by Duncan. During the banquet at Inverness, the king is seen to propose a toast, speaking the words 'Health to this household!'. Macbeth remains unmoved, absorbed in his thoughts, and the king glances at him indulgently. This does not necessarily happen in the play. Polanski subdues the sound of Duncan's toast so that we are aware of just how deeply Macbeth is ruminating on his projected plans.[7]

Duncan does not know what Macbeth is thinking – but we do, since we can hear him. This is our special insight into Macbeth's character, just as it is in Shakespeare. This is how we are drawn to Macbeth, as we were drawn to Rosemary – by the sharing of thoughts. This is how we are invited to engage with Macbeth, how we respond to him sympathetically. Shakespeare's text provides a template which Polanski amplifies with cinematic techniques.

This is best exemplified by Polanski's rendering one of the most famous scenes in the play, the vision of the dagger. In the play, on his way to murder Duncan, Macbeth has a vision of a bloodied dagger, an image that prompts one of the most well-known speeches in the play: 'Is this a dagger which I see before me?' (2.1.34).

Polanski's handling of this scene has also come under fire from some critics. On stage there can be no such visible dagger. Its existence is not seen, only known by Macbeth's description of it. In film, a director can go further. He or she can choose whether or not we share Macbeth's imaginings. In Polanski's film, the dagger is there in full view of the audience as well as Macbeth. For some critics this visual realisation of the dagger on screen suggested that Polanski had not quite managed to reconcile his Shakespearean

Fig. 9. 'Is this a dagger which I see before me?'.

source material with his cinematic expertise. For Forsyth, the superimposed image of a dagger in Macbeth's field of vision is too jarring, its artificiality emphasised by its 'sparkling with a Disney or washing-powder radiance' (2007: 288). To him, the blatant illustration of the dagger in the film epitomised his earlier reservations regarding Polanski's uncertain handling of the realism of film medium and the supernaturalism of Shakespeare; and he was not alone. David I. Grossvogel considered that showing the dagger on screen was one of many ways in which Shakespeare's 'character's complexity is diminished' by Polanski and Tynan, since, in insisting on such a projection, they did not seem to be trusting Shakespeare's language. The fact that Shakespeare has Macbeth express doubt as to the truth of his vision – '... art thou but / A dagger of the mind, a false creation / Proceeding from the heat-oppressèd brain' (2.1.38-40) – is, for Grossvogel a sign of the 'flickering sanity' of Shakespeare's character. Such lines as these are, for him, undermined in the film by Polanski's 'incontrovertible object' (1972: 49).

This scene, for these critics, becomes another example of Shakespeare's language being accorded a 'secondary' status where aspects of the supernatural are concerned, of Polanski's rendering of the play as 'unShakespearean'. This is not the case. Polanski is not mismanaging his Shakespeare source material. He is simply taking full advantage of his medium to amplify the inner life of Macbeth as presented by Shakespeare as he contemplates, and acts upon, that most deplorable of human sins. Jack J. Jorgens called this Polanski's ability to make 'the inner outer' (1977: 170). The 'inner' state is made 'outer' in the film by a literal illustration of what Macbeth is saying. For example, when he asks 'Thou sure and firm set earth / Hear not my steps, which way they walk, for fear / The very stones prate of my whereabouts' (2.2.57-9), the camera follows his gaze downward to his feet moving on the stones of the castle floor. His inward reflections are here accompanied by a literal realisation of his thinking.

Thus it is with the vision of the dagger; it is a literal realisation of Macbeth's inner state. Polanski does not rely entirely on such literal illustrations to grant us access to Macbeth's inner world. This is enhanced in the film by the use of voice-overs. While the soliloquies on stage are spoken aloud, cinema affords the luxury of a technology that allows us to be drawn in even further to Macbeth's state of mind. Those in the film that notice Macbeth 'rapt' do not know what he is thinking – but we do. We hear his inner voice say 'Is this a dagger which I see before me?' Only three lines of this famous meditation on the vision – almost all of which is retained in the screenplay – are actually spoken aloud. This voice-over technique allows the audience a direct, subjective participation in Macbeth's state of mind and is a means by which we can participate in Macbeth's vision, his darkest imagining.

Such an engagement with Macbeth is enhanced by his physical positioning in front of the camera during these scenes. Critics have noticed that he appears in profile in many shots in the film, placed 'at the edge of the frame, which renders the world as an object of his vision' (Mazierska, 2007:149). During this speech, Macbeth is to the left of the screen in profile with the dagger at the front and centre of the shot, enabling us to see it as clearly as he does; which is also the reason why it seems to sparkle and look 'Disney-like'. We have to have our attention drawn to the dagger, to look at it along with Macbeth and notice too, as he stretches his arm toward us, that it passes through the image. When not in profile, we stand with him. As the dagger moves toward Duncan's chamber, the camera is behind him and we are looking over his right shoulder. Then, with the camera, we follow him, almost alongside, as he says that the dagger 'marshall'st me the way that I was going / And such an instrument I was to use' (2.1.43-4). We share the vision and 'walk' with him as he approaches, looking down behind him as he draws his own dagger.

This use of the camera, accompanied by the voice-overs and the outer realisations of the inner thoughts of Macbeth, show Polanski to be exploiting the film medium as a means of showing the interior life of a character in ways that a stage play cannot, achieving what Kenneth S. Rothwell described as a 'convergence of consciousness [between Macbeth and the audience], heightened and intensified by the mesmerizing effect of the technicolor screen in the dark playhouse' (1993: 74). Where the theatre might exclude us from any direct participation in Macbeth's visions, film does not: and, since, in this film, we have been granted the insight into Macbeth's thoughts while he is 'rapt', so we are granted access to his visions. We are privy to the thoughts of this man who broods on the supernatural, who badly wants to believe in the existence of a numinous parallel world that can control and influence human matters. So badly, that he *wills* the dagger into existence. It does not appear of its own volition; and, given our subjective sharing of what goes on in his mind, we see it too, see him willing it to be real by reaching out and grasping for it.

The extent of our sympathetic engagement with Macbeth is seen in our sharing of these visions. We also see a vision of Fleance seizing the crown, the ghost of Banquo and his final visions invoked by the weird women. This vision of Fleance was added to the screenplay – there is no corresponding scene in Shakespeare. The purpose of this particular addition is for us to share one of Macbeth's 'terrible dreams / that shake [him] nightly' (3.2.20-1). As he lies down, Macbeth sees Fleance appear at the foot of his bed and reach for the crown, lifting it onto his own head. Then, in a visual echo of the murder of Duncan, Fleance takes an arrow and draws away Macbeth's bed cover, leaving the point of the dagger hovering over his exposed chest. He is unable to cry out, feeling Banquo's hand close over his mouth. This transforms into the hand of his wife and we see from her reaction that this is not a supernatural intrusion by her further admonition that this is one of the 'sorriest fancies' (3.2.10) to which he has lately been prone.

Lady Macbeth is here reminding us that there is an alternative viewpoint – that such a vision was not 'real' but experienced only by Macbeth. This idea that there are two realities, one of Macbeth's visions of the supernatural and one that shows us no such things exist is exemplified in the scene with Banquo's ghost. That only Macbeth can see the ghost is in keeping with Shakespeare's play. The text indicates that this vision is Macbeth's alone, that the clearly baffled guests are not privy to the sight of the ghost.

In film, this could be made explicit with multiple camera angles that create a collage of viewpoints showing those who can see the ghost and those who cannot.[8] However, in Polanski's film we share both Macbeth's vision of Banquo and experience his terror, whilst at the same time we are shown that, despite Macbeth's conviction, the ghost is not real.

All of this is achieved by the way the scene is played and staged. At the beginning, the use of the camera does not privilege Macbeth's insight. As the banquet starts, Macbeth offers to play 'the humble host' (3.4.4-5) and, after exchanging a glance with Ross as he enters, having just killed the murderers, toasts the absent Banquo. Throughout this beginning, the audience sees the empty stool between Ross and Lennox, who draw attention to it when they invite Macbeth to 'sit' (3.4.39). Macbeth approaches the stool, stands behind it, then walks away. Ross requests that he 'grace us with your royal company' (3.4.45), but receives in response a slight shrug from his king and the remark 'the table's full' even though he is assured that there is 'a place reserved' (3.4.46). We see the slightly puzzled expression on Macbeth's face and then in the next shot, realise that he can see someone seated next to Ross, a grey-hued man with his back to us. At this point, the action around the table is stilled, the characters are frozen, and the camera slowly draws toward the figure. The shot culminates in the white face of Banquo turning slowly toward us. This is a visual manifestation of Macbeth's growing realisation that something is amiss, an ominous thrum of the soundtrack providing a means for us to feel Macbeth's growing unease and terror. The shock of the moment is punctuated by the sound of his cup falling to the floor, an aural reminder of the clattering of Duncan's crown as it fell to the floor during his murder. Despite the pleading of his wife, whose delivery of the lines in an urgent, anxious tone heightens the sense of fear, we are drawn to the unblinking eyes of Macbeth as he stares at the ghost of Banquo. From this point on, the viewpoint is all his – and ours too. He is surrounded by rising mist, enclosing him, and us, in a tenebrous agitation, as he faces the 'gory locks' (3.4.51) of the bloodied Banquo. After watching the figure reach out toward him, we hear Macbeth's cry of 'Thou canst not say I did this' (3.4.50) and, from then on, the camera does not show the empty stool. We see Ross rise from his seat and Lady Macbeth hasten forward to entreat everyone to stay – and we only see Ross at the front of the screen, not the vacant place at the table. By the time the camera pans around to the stool again, we shortly learn from Macbeth that the ghost of Banquo has left his seat and is lurching toward him. We see the transparent figure of Banquo moving forward, and on the left a massive fireplace can be seen in full, its tall chimney and flames providing a visual reminder of the furnaces of hell, casting an otherworldly glow behind the staggering ghost as it reaches out to Macbeth.

Fig. 10. 'Hence, horrible shadow! Unreal mockery, hence!'

This is another of those queasy moments when our senses are charged by the crossing over from benign sociable togetherness over into the unreal, fevered imagination of Macbeth. Polanski here again creates that 'twilight' feeling that leads us to think something supernatural is amiss and enhances the feeling with the imagery of hell. Such techniques enable us to engage with Macbeth in this scene on a visceral level. Yet, despite the pull on our own emotions as we absorb Macbeth's terror, we are also coolly presented with the viewpoints of others. The scene is also marked by the presence of an alternative reality, one which undercuts this supernatural experience of Macbeth. The very appearance of the ghost is a case in point. Kliman noted that the manifestation of Banquo's spirit is subject to Macbeth's own imaginings. He has been told by the First Murderer that his throat was cut and there were 'twenty trenchèd gashes on his head' (3.4.27). That is not what we have seen earlier – we saw Banquo struck down with an axe in his back and fall face first into water. Yet, as Kliman observes, 'when Macbeth sees Banquo, the ghost appears as the murderer described him, not as he actually died'

(2004: 202). The ghost of Banquo is, therefore, a projection of Macbeth's mind, it is not 'real': 'Mental not supernatural forces account for the ghost' (2004: 204).

Throughout the scene, Polanski presents us with discrepancies between the way Macbeth sees things and how they really are. That Banquo's ghost is an illusion is endorsed in the film, as it is in the play, by the others' responses. Lady Macbeth rebukes him: 'Why do you make such faces? / When all's done you look but on a stool' (3.4.67-8). As Macbeth begins to recover his composure he wonders aloud why the sight of Banquo's ghost has left him white-faced with fear but has not affected anyone else. Why have 'such sights' (3.4.115) not shaken the others? To which the response is, 'What sights, my lord?' (3.4.117). Placed in the mind of the audience is the conviction that this was something only Macbeth saw. So while we have the insight into his mind and we share his visions, his conviction that the supernatural is real, we have also been shown, in this scene, palpable evidence of a different reality.

Fig. 11. 'What sights, my lord?'

This idea is also explored in the second encounter with the weird women. This scene has gained in notoriety due to its presentation of a coven of women all of whom are nude. Such a sight has led to the scene being regarded by critics in the light of the emergent politics of the 1960s. The on-screen image of a group of nude women of various ages has been referred to by Deanne Williams as 'an unappealing image of first-wave feminist sisterhood' (2004: 153).This evocation of a burgeoning feminist freedom, apparently expressed by the nudity of the women reflects the larger preoccupation of many critics with interpreting this scene in the light of 1960s counterculture. Deats sees the visions invoked by the women as 'not magical incantations, but hallucinations induced by psychedelic drugs' (1986: 87). Forsyth also made the connection between Macbeth's drinking of the potion and the desire 'to get high' and the subsequent visions leading to an inevitable reminder 'of a California LSD experience' (2007: 289).

The problem with such interpretations is that they are remnants from the time when the film was widely viewed by some as a response to the Manson murders, when the lifestyle of the hippie 'family' was implied by the press to have been a contributing factor, with drug-taking and 'alternative' lifestyles being seen as conversant, if not synonymous, with witchcraft and black magic.This tendency to read into such scenes a contemporary preoccupation with altered states is not necessarily inaccurate – we have seen from the scene with Banquo's ghost that Polanski creates an atmosphere conducive to create a heightened awareness. In this second meeting with the women, however, this is not the case. As we have seen, in Polanski's film, the weird woman are far from being hallucinations. From the very beginning, they are underplayed, seen as part of the landscape. Here, this second visit to the women is no exception, as the youngest leads Macbeth down some steps and into an underground cavern, literally bringing him into the earth.This makes the fact of their nudity not an expression of a new wave of feminist freedom, but an underscoring of their link to the landscape, being in their 'natural' state.[9]

Such sights serve to remind us that these are not mystical wraiths performing a ritual in a fog-shrouded eldritch landscape, but a group of nude women, throwing things into a pot and chanting.They are shown to put in exactly what they say – eyes, tongues, snakes, liver and lips – not vaguely unidentifiable props. As Rothwell noted, 'We actually see "liver of blaspheming jew"; it is dangled right before our eyes ... for all the world like some closed-circuit TV medical school instructional unit' (1973: 74). Such things are given a supernatural interpretation, once again, only by Macbeth himself.The potion he drinks works, gives him prophetic visions, not because of any inherent power in it, but because he *believes* that it will.

As with the Banquo scene, Polanski presents us with an alternate viewpoint. It is very telling that, in drinking the potion, Macbeth does not summon up any demons, even though, when the women ask him 'if thou'd'st hear it from our mouths / or from our masters' (4.1.76-7) this would seem to be moving the film into genuinely occult and mystical territory; but, when Macbeth chooses the 'masters', it is not with a demonic form that he communicates – nor even, as Shakespeare's play has, 'an armèd head' (4.1.82). As he looks into the water, he sees himself and it is his double that speaks.

Fig. 12. 'Beware the Thane of Fife' - Macbeth's own reflection utters the prophecies.

Even the advice he is given by this doppelgänger ('Beware the Thane of Fife') tells him what he has already suspected. Earlier in the film Macbeth has already expressed his suspicions regarding Macduff, noting to his wife that he 'denies his person / At our great bidding' (3.4.129-30). So when he hears the words of his lookalike he acknowledges 'thou hast harped my fear aright' (4.1.88). His further visions are also seen in the film as a reflection of his own suspicions and concerns. The image of the child is not bloodied, as in the play (4.1.91), but when it recites the words 'none of woman born / Shall harm Macbeth' (4.1.94-5) the speech and image is blended with that of Macbeth's own as he echoes the words. This has the effect of blurring the lines somewhat between whether the words are spoken by an independent spirit, or, as is implied in the film, they arise from Macbeth himself.

That the visions are the products of Macbeth's own mind is also shown in the manifestation of the third apparition. In Shakespeare's play, this is a crowned child with a tree in its hand (4.1.99). In Polanski's film this apparition becomes Malcolm and Donalbain who are not children, but exhibit childish behaviour, clapping, giggling and speaking in juvenile voices. This undermines their appearance as demonic spectres, since they are seen by Macbeth as childish and therefore, to his mind, not at all threatening. It is they who utter the words 'Macbeth shall never vanquish'd be until / Great Birnam Wood to high Dunsinane Hill / Shall come against him' (4.1.107-9). The fact that Macbeth sees two people he knows, whose threat is diminished by puerile posturing, and not a single mystical spirit, underscores the fact that these visions emanate from his own imagination and not from a supernatural source.

Even when he sees the images of Banquo and his descendants it is also only a reflection of his own fear, expressed throughout the film that Banquo will be 'father to a line of kings' (3.1.59). The sight of the laughing Banquo is a reminder of the first encounter of the two of them with the women, when they laughed at Banquo's teasing 'You shall be king / And Thane of Cawdor' (1.3.86-7). This laughter, and the associated recollection of the earlier encounter with the women, is an aural reminder that what we are seeing is a reflection of Macbeth's own mind, not an objective vision.

In Shakespeare's play, this scene concludes with the women dancing, then vanishing before Macbeth's eyes (4.1.147). In Polanski's film, there is no such vision. Macbeth simply wakes on the floor of the cavern and they have gone. We have not seen them melt away or vanish – and neither has he, although he assumes that that have, in the manner of all spirits, ridden away on the air ('infected be the air whereon they ride!': 4.1.153): but so powerfully does he believe what they have told him of his invincibility that, on his return, he extinguishes a burning taper with his bare hand. He has indeed 'almost forgot the taste of fears' (5.5.9).

Only at the end do we get a glimmer of Macbeth's vulnerability, the return of that fear. This is when he is faced with the realisation of the final prophecies. The first, concerning Birnam Wood has come in for some criticism regarding its presentation in the film. The sequence where it appears that Birnam Wood has, indeed, come to Dunsinane was described by Petersen as a 'surprisingly inept realization' (1994: 52). This typifies an expectation that, somehow, with all the cinematic resources at his disposal, Polanski might have found a way to present this scene 'realistically'; that, perhaps, the viewer might be treated to the sight of Birnam Wood actually seeming to move.

This would be to concede that the story of the film is one of supernatural events, when, as we have seen, Polanski believes no such thing. They are only in the perception of the characters, and especially Macbeth. Polanski retains the lines spoken by the Messenger that '... anon, *methought* / The wood began to move' (5.5.34-5: my emphasis) to show that it *looks* as if the wood is moving. The fact that it is not, is underscored by a small change to Shakespeare's play. In the screenplay, Malcolm's instructions to his men to 'hew him down a bough / And bear't before him' (5.4.4-5) have been put into the mouths of two soldiers as a commentary on what they have seen: 'Thereby they shadow / The number of their host, and make discovery / Err in report of them' (5.4.5-7). This has the effect of undermining further the incident as a rendering of a supernatural occurrence. By having the two soldiers underscore the practice as a military tactic, it makes it more obvious what we, the audience is meant to see – a line of men carrying tree branches approaching the castle and not the illusion of a moving forest.

This is also the moment in the film when Macbeth himself begins to see things as they really are. Since we are privy to Macbeth's visions, Polanski could have taken the decision to show the approach of the forest as a special effect. This time, for the first time, he sees it for what it is – men carrying branches; but though he muses that he begins 'to be aweary of the sun / And wish the estate of the world were now undone' (5.5.49-50), he soon rallies. After all, this is one of two pronouncements given by his visions that tell him he is invincible. At the end of the film, he takes refuge in the second prophecy of his invincibility – that he cannot be killed by man 'of woman born' (5.7.43). Grossvogel disapproved of what he saw as Polanski's Macbeth having a 'naive belief' in such prophecies, believing that they undercut Shakespeare's presentation of Macbeth's resigned fatalism in the final scenes (1972: 50). For Jorgens, in the film 'Shakespeare's balance of sympathy and condemnation is absent at the end' (1977: 172). This is not so. This Macbeth still fights with bravado ('I will not yield / To kiss the ground before young Malcolm's feet': 5.7.57-8) even when faced with the reality of his impending defeat. When he finds out that he is not protected by even this second charm, he falters – 'it hath cowed my better part of man' (5.7.48) – and finally acknowledges the truth: '...be these juggling fiends no more believed / That palter with us in a double sense' (5.7.49-50).

In Macbeth's demise, we share one final vision. When he is killed, beheaded by Macduff, his trunk clatters down the steps, which we see, and then we watch as his head is seized and placed on a pike. Suddenly, the camera angle is low, travelling quickly through the crowds who jeer and shout. We are seeing through the eyes of the severed head of Macbeth, travelling on one last journey with him.

As far as horror is concerned that last, shared viewpoint through the eyes of a corpse is macabre enough. It epitomises the extent to which we have shared the visions of Macbeth. Yet, throughout the film, our sympathetic engagement with this monster has been compromised by the uncomfortable realisation that his evil does not come from an otherworldly source. Since Polanski eschews any evidence of the supernatural in the play except that which is mediated through the visions of Macbeth, there remains a discomfiting sense that, in sharing his thoughts and his visions, we become complicit in Macbeth's machinations. We, too, are the 'murdering ministers' (1.5.47). In this subjective sharing of Macbeth's deepest desires Polanski is exploiting one of the foundational constituents of horror: the sharing of the human capacity for evil.

The diminution of the supernatural in the film functions as part of the larger intention to show that power, the desire for it and the means by which it is obtained, remain exclusively in the human domain. By eschewing the supernatural in the play as the source of the horror and explicitly choosing not to use those otherworldly elements to explore evil, Polanski locates the horror firmly in the realm of human frailty.

We are given enough hints in the film to show the primal urge beneath the apparently civilised exterior that motivates him to such brutality. This rapacity, concealed by an ostensibly civilised veneer, enables us to consider it a horror film, since Polanski was exploring a theme he had previously presented in *Rosemary's Baby* – that is, using horror codes and conventions to make a comment on the evil inherent in human ambition. An evil that is nurtured by the society they inhabit – in the case of *Macbeth*, the tribal world of feudal warfare. In this rough and ready setting of unrefined domesticity with its buildings exposed to, and damaged by, the elements, Polanski was able to hold a mirror to the contemporary society by presenting a world where violence is barely fettered beneath the homespun, creating a twilight world of dread.

This connects the film with developments in the contemporary horror genre, and it manifests itself in this context in which Macbeth's crimes are played out. There are certainly a number of Shakespeareans, such as Kliman, who have recognised that Polanski's film shows that 'society, rather than the supernatural ... determines the outcome' of the play (2004: 191). The idea was also beginning to be explored in the wider horror genre of the late 1960s and 1970s, whereby horror provided a commentary on contemporary social mores and politics in films such as George A. Romero's *Night of the Living Dead*. That this is also a key feature of Polanski's *Macbeth* can be seen in the interpretation, not just of Macbeth himself, but of two other characters in the play, Ross and Malcolm, as we shall see in Chapter 4.

FOOTNOTES

1.   The aftermath of the murder even concludes with some knocking at the door which, while also present in Shakespeare's play, at one point is here presented in the classic Grand Guignol tradition: that is, three loud knocks, a sound said to preface every performance at the notorious Théâtre du Grand Guignol, Paris; see Skal, 1994: 58.

2.   In fact, Polanski specifically sets the film in the year 1067; see Parker, 1993: 186.

3.   Another example of Polanski's practice of being involved in the minutiae of the film-making process is his insistence upon such props as the costumes looking authentic for the period; see Parker, 1993: 186.

4.   Though not in one continuous shot, but more of a 'time lapse' effect; see Jorgens, 1977: 161.

5.   Lorne M. Buchman notes that the long shot of the landscape is disturbed by a close-up shot of 'a crooked stick ... bisecting the picture'. For him, this is to define a space on the screen – the close-up – as a 'space for strange enactments' (1991:70).

6.   The digging, the rope and the dagger are also Renaissance 'emblems of despair'; see Crowl, 1992: 24.

7.   See Buchman for a reading of this scene in terms of Polanski's use of close-up and voice-over (1991: 75).

8.   As does, for example, Orson Welles, who makes a distinction between what the guests see and what Macbeth himself sees by having the ghost appear, in isolation, at the end of an empty table when he is the object of Macbeth's gaze. But when the guests are seen, there is a full table of guests and only one empty chair.

9.   Such things – the connection between the landscape and the nudity – are more in keeping with Gerald Gardner, whose book *Witchcraft Today*, published in 1954, is associated with the modern revival of witchcraft.

CHAPTER 4: POLANSKI'S *MACBETH* AS SOCIAL COMMENTARY – 'NONE CAN CALL OUR POWER TO ACCOUNT'

In *Rosemary's Baby*, Polanski managed to take the conventions of Hammer horror – the Gothic world of demons as goat-headed men, of magic spells and covens – and place them in a modern world of coffee machines and Christmas shopping. From the old, he fashioned the new. In *Macbeth*, Polanski took this further. He overlaid Shakespeare's play with the old Gothic bright red blood-and-guts and, instead of just presenting it in a modern world, he chose the landscape of a feudal nation, and the inner world of Macbeth, to create a film that was a commentary on that modernity.

What consolidates this is Polanski's use of Shakespeare's play, which shows us that a violent tendency is not Macbeth's alone, but is also symptomatic of the society he inhabits. This aspect of some horror films, that they functioned as a commentary on contemporary social anxieties of the late 1960s and 1970s, is widely recognised (e.g. Wood, 1984: 164-200) and indeed it has been noted by Peter Hutchings that Polanski's own film can be seen as one of these early innovative horrors (2008: 160-1) given its rendering of the events in Shakespeare's play as an appraisal on the social mores of the time. Polanski, with a few deft touches to Shakespeare's play was one of the originators of this new type of horror that emerged at the turn of the decade.

'THE WORTHY THANE OF ROSS'

As with *Rosemary's Baby*, Polanski took the features of the current horror and refreshed them for a new generation of the genre. Two of the ways that Polanski achieved this have already been explored: in the use of violence, its graphic presentation, but also the fear of it; and the presentation of the supernatural which leads to the realisation that in the film evil itself is a social, not mystical, phenomenon. Polanski also conveyed this latter idea through something that many Shakespeareans spotted in the film shortly after it was released. In the interpretation of the character of another ambitious man, one with no real loyalty to anyone other than himself, Polanski finally cast into a new and, then, ultra-modern shape, the Shakespeare text and reinvented it as new horror.

Fig. 13. Ross, the 'smirking sociopath'.

This particular interpretation makes the film much more a part of the cinematic horror genre since it relates to developments in contemporary horror film-making. Initially, a number of Shakespeareans interpreted the film in terms of its literary, rather than cinematic heritage. Critics such as Deanne Williams identified Polanski's *Macbeth* as reflecting the social and political conditions of the 1960s as expressed in the theatrical arts,[1] in particular, the disillusion that had manifested itself as a result of the failure of the political ideals that had offered such promise for the future. These were epitomised in the theatre in such works as the so-called 'Angry Young Man' dramas of John Osborne, or the bleak existentialism of Samuel Beckett. Polanski's film, for critics such as Williams, reflected that same disillusion.

Such disaffection was not only manifested in the British theatre. As we have seen, it had started to appear in American horror films of the late 1960s, epitomised, to use one example, by George A. Romero's *Night of the Living Dead*. The lack of positive change in social and political conditions after an era of optimism had forced film directors such as Romero to face and explore an unpleasant truth: that the failure to create a just and fair world through the reform of the larger institutions of society was due to the fact that those same institutions, and the society they were deemed to protect, nurtured not goodness but self-interest. This, in turn, was leading some people to act for their own benefit and not with regard to others.

So while the Shakespeareans are correct in identifying that same disenchantment as being present in Polanski's film, it did not arise purely from the theatrical traditions. Instead, it emerged as part of this new trend in horror cinema, which took the idea further and explored the inevitable outcome of such a preoccupation with self-interest: the idea that evil is not a manifestation of supernatural, Gothic forces, but a social phenomenon.

In Polanski's *Macbeth*, this is epitomised in the character of Ross (played by John Stride).[2] In the film, he is very different from in Shakespeare's play (Rothwell, 1983: 50-5). Originally, he is a minor character with very little dialogue. His role is aptly summarised by the line, 'My countryman: but yet I know him not' (4.3.160), expressing what is essentially his anonymity.

Ross, in Polanski's film, is afforded no such anonymity. He does not simply provide some local colour in the background but, from the very outset, is brought to the forefront in his opening scenes, to embody Polanski's social commentary. As in the play, after the first news of Macbeth's victories, it is Ross who appears in front of Duncan with Cawdor strapped to a board, dragged behind his horse. Polanski uses this image of the two men together, one of whom is a traitor, to provide the audience with a visual clue as to Ross' own flexible loyalties which will be revealed as the film progresses. His presence is also marked by the delivery of his lines. Stride says his piece in a clear, ringing voice outlining Macbeth's heroic victories and Cawdor's betrayal; but there is a slightly disconcerting note in Stride's tone, ever so slightly sycophantic. It marginally undercuts his triumphant account of the battle lost and won, making him sound a little *too* earnest in his loyalty to the victors.

Polanski's visual and aural presentation of the character of Ross in his first scene announces him as one who follows whoever is on the winning side and happy to help dispose of anyone that stands in their way. This is what he does over the course of the film, first supporting Macbeth and then switching allegiance to the equally morally suspect Malcolm. Such a sub-plot is evidence of Polanski's successful collaboration with Tynan, whose encyclopaedic knowledge was brought to bear on the development of the role of Ross; in this instance, the work of a Victorian schoolmaster called M. F. Libby, who, as early as 1893, conducted a literary analysis of the character and found within him the scope for evil (Rothwell, 2004: 151). Polanski and Tynan enlarged upon this literary model, but not by making any adjustments to Shakespeare's text. Instead, Polanski's direction makes the same point. Ross is never very far away from the significant action in the film and you can always see him. In some scenes, if you look away momentarily from the main action on the screen in front of you, Ross is lurking in the background, as is his wont in the play; but there are occasions when the attention is subtly drawn toward him. As Lady Macbeth and her husband enter the room where the revels are continuing after the banquet, to the right of the grooms dancing, there is Ross, arms folded, looking on. In the following scene where the Macbeths plot to murder Duncan, Ross is not immediately obvious. The conspiring couple are filmed in close up, so very little background is in view; but as soon as the camera pulls away when Duncan offers to dance with Lady Macbeth, there, in the background, watching the action closely is Ross. At any point during that scene, if you glance away from the dancing king and the duplicitous lady, your eyes alight on another, equally treacherous individual.

Scenes such as these led to Kenneth S. Rothwell's memorable description of Stride's portrayal of Ross as that of a 'smirking sociopath' and his presence on screen as a 'silent movie ... that remains nested within the framework of the talking movie about Macbeth' (2004: 151). 'Silent movie' is an apt analogy here. Ross' silent (but very visible) presence in the background shows that, to achieve a reading of the character as a self-interested sycophant, he does not need to state his intentions. He only needs to be seen in the proximity of people of influence at crucial moments in the shifting balance of power.

This concept of Ross' silence is present throughout the film. There is no additional dialogue added to the play. Stride as Ross speaks only Shakespeare's words; but his performance is tinged by a multiplicity of facial expressions that load those words with extra meaning. Such a strategy is effective since, with the medium of cinema, the sheer size of the screen allows an audience to read those silent expressions to an extent that would not be necessarily immediately apparent to an audience in a darkened theatre auditorium. The scene in which Ross intercepts the funeral procession of Duncan is a good example. Here Shakespeare's dialogue is given a pointed nuance by Stride's expression, and by the response to him from Bayler as Macduff. In the play, Shakespeare's dialogue is fairly straightforward here, information concerning the funeral and coronation being passed to the audience via these two men. In the film, the scene has an added depth provided by the subtle modulations of expression from the actors.

It is played as if Ross were asking obvious questions, ones to which Macduff knows he has the answers and therefore making him overtly suspicious of Ross' motives and correspondingly wary and brief in his answers. His response to Ross' greeting 'How goes the world, Macduff?' is a sharp 'Why? See you not?' (2.4.21) and he seems reluctant to speak to him. To Ross' question 'Is it known who did this more than bloody deed?' (2.4.22), Macduff offers the non-committal 'Those that Macbeth hath slain' (2.4.23) with an expression that reads 'and well you know this'. To Ross' expression of apparent sympathy, he relents and tells him that Malcolm and Donalbain have fled the country. The camera switches to a close-up of Ross, whose face assumes a casual air of studied indifference. His remark that, as a result of their absence, Macbeth will be crowned changes from a merely expository line for the audience's benefit to the onset of a plan that can be seen, in full close up, formulating in his mind. It just requires him to quickly check whether Macduff will be there ('Will you to Scone?': 2.4.35) and then make a polite, but hasty retreat. That his motives have been anything but altruistic is shown in Macduff's final comment – 'May you see things well done there' (2.4.37) – that are uttered so warily as to illustrate his own suspicion that Ross is hastening away to support the winning side.[3]

The response of Macduff is indicative that other characters are used to reinforce the duplicitous nature of the character that Polanski and Tynan have formed and, again, it requires no additional dialogue – sometimes merely a silent stare. The reaction of Banquo to Ross is particularly telling. When Macbeth is crowned at Scone, he is raised on the shield bearing the robes and accoutrements of his new office, lifted by a group of thanes that include Ross and Banquo. Standing next to one another, Ross is the first to cry out – and loudly enough for the words to echo – 'Hail Macbeth! Hail, King of Scotland!' As the cry is taken up by the other thanes, the camera remains fixed on both Banquo and Ross. The former, at Ross' cry, turns to him and fixes him with a cold, unblinking stare. So much so, that we see the smile slowly fall from Ross' face and his confidence momentarily falter.

Only momentarily, though. Banquo's obvious distaste at Ross' proclaimed loyalty implies that, given the opportunity, Ross would gladly assist in any action against *him*. Having presented Ross with such a motive, Polanski and Tynan exploit Shakespeare's text by making use of a silent character in Shakespeare's play to reinforce Ross as the usurper's henchman of choice. In the film, Ross is cast as someone simply called the 'Third Murderer'. In Shakespeare's play, Macbeth interviews two murderers for the killing of Banquo; but when the murder is played out on stage, an unnamed third murderer appears on the scene. The explanation for this appearance is given in the text when the First Murderer asks the third man what he is doing there and receives the response that he is there at Macbeth's instigation.

In the film this motive of sending Ross along to ensure that the job is done is given a more solid realisation. When Macbeth interviews the two murderers one of them at least is reluctant to perform the deed, namely the younger of the two men (Andrew McCulloch). That he is the first man's son is indicated in the film by Macbeth's referring to Banquo's 'having bowed you to the grave' – indicating the first man (Michael Balfour) – then, on the line 'and beggared yours forever' (3.1.89-90), he points in the direction of the younger man, thus pointing out the relationship between the two. This young man attempts to interrupt, to protest, but is silenced by his father and by Macbeth, the former indicating behind the king's back that his son should be going along with everything. Given such hesitation, it is hardly surprising, then, that Macbeth should distrust them and send someone to oversee their appointed task – and it is equally unsurprising in the film that such a man turns out to be Ross.

Ross performs his duties ably in this instance. It is as well he is there since the two murderers are clumsy, crude in their handling of weapons and their amateurish scuffling against the professional soldier, Banquo. In the mêlée, Fleance is able to mount a horse and get away. Ross chases after him, and is stopped only by an arrow from Banquo that fells his horse. Interestingly, Ross does not continue the chase on foot. That he does not go all the way to fulfil Macbeth's desires is a rather subtle rendition of the mercenary nature of Ross' loyalty. What he does, he does for reward; and when he does not receive it, he moves on to serve someone who will. That Ross does not truly serve Macbeth, but only wants to be on what he deems the winning side, is seen by his defection to Malcolm when he misses out on a promotion. For his part in the disposal of Banquo, Banquo's murderers and the Macduffs, Ross stands expectantly with a group of thanes on the battlements of the castle, as Macbeth watches his men deserting him to 'mingle with the English epicures' (5.3.8). Holding the chain of office passed to him by Lennox, one of the deserters, Macbeth surveys the waiting thanes and then, impulsively, places the chain around the neck of Seyton (Noel Davies). The men leave and Ross remains, looking resplendently villainous in black leather and chains, glancing across to the defecting thanes, his silence and his expression betraying his thoughts. The next time we see Ross, he is approaching the English camp.

At the end of the film the screenplay retains some lines of Macbeth that make reference to his former followers having deserted him when he laments that the English army is stuffed 'with those that should be ours' (5.5.5). It is Ross' actions that are singled out to epitomise this. Macbeth, boasting that he is invincible during his final fight with Macduff, throws away his axe. We see it strike the helmet of one of the soldiers and as it falls, the soldier is revealed to be Ross. He, who at the beginning of the film was quite literally giving Macbeth a 'leg up' if only initially onto his horse, has entered the castle as one of Malcolm's invading army. The camera focuses on Stride as the helmet falls, and we see him physically and mentally momentarily unbalanced; but, typically, not for long. When Macbeth is beheaded, it is Ross who hands the crown to Malcolm and raises the cry of 'Hail! King of Scotland!'

The fact that it is Ross who crowns the new king supports Polanski's contention in the film that social and political institutions are not universal stable entities, but are subject to the whims and desire for gratification of those who supposedly have the larger interests of humankind in mind. This idea is rendered in the fact that Ross does not switch loyalties to someone of morally unimpeachable character, but rather to Polanski's version of Malcolm (Stephan Chase). Whereas in Shakespeare's play the future king is presented as an ideal candidate to rule a country, having the necessary altruism and godly virtues to preserve and protect the best interests of his subjects – expressed in his heroic speech in Act 4 – Polanski and Tynan do not retain any of Malcolm's virtues in their screenplay. Ross has thus not changed allegiance to a leader who demonstrates any redeeming virtues, but merely exchanged one morally dubious ruler for another.

That Malcolm is not any better a model of virtuous kingship is reinforced in the film by the screenplay being cut in such a way that he is presented throughout as a contrast to any model of gentlemanly virtue – in his response to disloyalty and in his own ambition, shown in his attitude to Macbeth as a potential rival for the crown. When the disgraced Thane of Cawdor, after impassively uttering 'Long live the king', throws himself from the battlements, Malcolm's comment here, as in the play, is the line 'Nothing in his life / Became him like the leaving it' (1.4.7-8). In Shakespeare's play, this is spoken in the context of a longer speech whereby Malcolm extols upon Cawdor's deathbed confession of disloyalty and pleads for forgiveness. In the play, Cawdor repents, and Malcolm forgives. As Polanski and Tynan have removed these lines from the screenplay what we hear instead is a very stark assessment of Cawdor's character. Since we do not hear of any deathbed confession, that single line delivered by Malcolm has the unpleasant subtext of 'he got what he deserved', with an edge of 'and we are better off without him'. The effect is to remove all elements of humility, not just from Cawdor on his deathbed, but Malcolm himself.

This lack of humility is present elsewhere. Polanski adds some business that marks Malcolm as not being the wholesome model of virtue presented by Shakespeare. It is made clear by Polanski from the outset that Macbeth and Malcolm do not get on well. At the beginning of the film, when the bloodied soldier is recounting Macbeth's victories, 'Donalbain is as delighted as Duncan' by the account, 'but Malcolm scowls' (Kliman, 1998: 134).[1] The motive for Macbeth's being persuaded by his wife to commit murder is built upon this idea that the two men are not comrades. In fact, in the screenplay, this marks the turning point at which Macbeth moves from merely contemplating murder to actually committing it. It is the action of Malcolm that drives it (See Crowl, 1992: 27). After the feast, Lady Macbeth seeks out her husband who is brooding over the matter of murder. He tells her that he does not wish to go ahead with their plans ('We will proceed no further in this business': 1.7.31). His tearful wife rebukes him for raising her hopes and then exhibiting such unmanly cowardice ('When you durst do it, then you were a man': 1.7.49). Agitated, Macbeth turns away from her and goes to refresh his drink. As he starts to pour wine into his own cup, another is thrust in front of him. It is Malcolm's. Macbeth pours the wine into both their cups. Malcolm raises his and says, with a deadpan expression, 'Hail, Thane of Cawdor'. As Sara M. Deats (1986: 91) noted, it is such 'smug vaunting' of Malcolm, treating Macbeth 'like a common steward' that changes Macbeth's mind. It brings to mind the sight of the servant refilling Macbeth's own cup during the meal – Malcolm treats Macbeth at that moment like that servant. He drinks from his own cup, ponders this second assault on his manhood, then returns to his wife and asks 'If we should fail?' (1.7.59).

In all of these aspects of the character, Polanski shows us a side of Malcolm not present in Shakespeare's play, as a man who does not possess 'wise prudence and moral discernment' (Deats, 1986: 91). This is also emphasised in the final scenes of the film. We do not get to see Malcolm as King, radiating goodness. Once he has the crown there is no final shot of him, resplendently gracious in his new authority. Nor is there any speech about the restoration of right and the rule 'by the grace of Grace' (5.7.102) as there is in Shakespeare's play, where there is no doubt that right has been restored. Instead, there is a rather troublesome conclusion (notwithstanding the final scene involving Donalbain, which will be discussed later) and no satisfying sense of closure in the film, as there can be in Shakespeare's play; but this kind of ambiguity best befits the developments in the horror genre that were emerging at this time.

This is because of the person who gives the crown to Malcolm – Ross. It is Ross who picks it up from the fallen Macbeth and presents it to Malcolm. It is also Ross who is the first to hail the new king, just as he was the first, and loudest, to hail Macbeth at his coronation. By seeing Ross in full view, and listening to the echo of his proclamation, the audience has a visual and aural reminder of the occasions when he did the same for Macbeth. The fact that Ross wipes Macbeth's bloodstains off the crown before giving it to the new king means that such a gesture is not, as it might be in a theatrical performance of Shakespeare's play, a symbol of the crown being cleansed of any moral taint. In Polanski's film, it is the gesture of the opportunist, wiping away his association with one who lost, in order to show loyalty to the new opening that has just presented itself. In this small gesture is an indication that Ross functions as an emblem of what Bernice W. Kliman called Polanski's 'notion of a diseased society' (1998: 142).

The fact that Ross is even around to crown Malcolm acts as another telling piece of social commentary. As Deats points out, it shows Ross' success in all his enterprises. Watching him hand the crown to Malcolm indicates that he has not been punished for changing allegiances, being at the coronation of both kings. This, in turn, leads to the realisation, that 'any regime that includes the moral chameleon Ross among its trusted supporters is stained and doomed' (1986: 91). Not a stain that is so easily wiped away.

Ross' change of loyalties is the culmination of Polanski's presentation of the character as a commentary on the society he inhabits. It might not seem that way at first. Ross' role in the film as Macbeth's supporter can be more akin to the tradition in action films whereby the villain always has a number of black-clad loyal henchmen prepared to do the dirty work. Kliman has identified that the film contains not just Ross, but 'Numerous willing partners' who 'abet Macbeth in crime' (2004: 200). However, such a creation as Ross in the film is still very much in keeping with the horror tradition, an indicator of the new direction in which the genre was going. Ross' silence makes one more telling point. We have seen in *Rosemary's Baby* and *Macbeth* how there is a strong belief in the supernatural, even if that belief is not realised in the film. Ross epitomises this. The screen version of Ross is unencumbered by even any *thought* of the supernatural and its influence. In fact, Polanski and Tynan cut from the play the one and only reference Ross makes to supernatural events. Shakespeare's Ross speaks to an Old Man before the funeral procession of the portents following Duncan's murder (2.4.1-20). He is troubled by an unnatural darkness that has apparently settled in the wake of the king's death, and that Duncan's own horses 'broke their stalls', reverting to their wild, untamed state and, as he witnessed, they 'ate each other' (2.4.18). In Polanski's film those lines have been excised, thus removing any association of the supernatural with the character. In the film, he is not shown as witnessing such events and is tellingly silent on the matter.

Such a silence, illustrating the materialism of Ross, serves as a rather maudlin take on human nature. It posits no redeeming features whatsoever by distilling the essence of the film into one clear message. In Ross' silence regarding the supernatural can be seen that there is no larger spiritual dimension that can influence his actions – no storms and portents, or weird sisters. Only his own ambitions motivate him. In terms of horror, this is an extension of the idea that was first explored in *Rosemary's Baby* that true horror derives from people's desires and not as the result of any 'supernatural soliciting' (1.3.131). Evil emerges, not from numinous beings directing affairs, but from the self-interested actions of human beings themselves.

This is the aspect of *Macbeth* that places the film firmly in the realm of contemporary horror, since, in the self-serving Ross, Polanski was able to express a very contemporary anxiety. Namely, that growing disillusion with the larger institutions that were set up supposedly to protect the people they were built to serve. In Ross, Polanski demonstrates in one fell swoop how the operation of those institutions may be subject to the whims of the self-serving individual with no thought to the greater good but their own immediate gratification; and the end result is not the hoped-for social improvement, but the conduct of evil.

This realisation – that a society and its institutions are only as altruistic as the people that serve them (expressed here in the character of Ross and the underlying story of his changing allegiance from one bad ruler to another) – was in tune with a recognised discontent with the post-hippie/flower power era in the late 1960s and early 1970s. A generation who felt that they had initiated permanent social change found that nothing was different. It created an anger that was expressed in the British theatre, but the full implications of it were explored in the American cinema where, according to George A. Romero, 'There was a good deal of a sort of anger ... we thought we had changed the world ... And all of a sudden it wasn't any better.'[5] This disillusionment would become a defining characteristic of the horror cinema of the era.

FOOTNOTES

1. See 'Mick Jagger Macbeth'. *Shakespeare Survey: 'Macbeth' and its Afterlife.* Vol. 57. Ed. Peter Holland. Cambridge: CUP, 2004, 145-58.
2. Sometimes spelled by Shakespeare critics as 'Rosse' as it is in the Shakespeare First Folio of 1623, but I am here using 'Ross' as it is in the screenplay.
3. See Kliman, 1998: 140 for a detailed account of Polanski's development of this scene through the various drafts of the screenplay.
4. Kliman noted that, in the reformatting of the film from cinema to 'boxy' VHS (2004: 208), this shot of Malcolm and Donalbain had been cut off. It has since been restored in the widescreen DVD format.
5. From an interview in *Birth of the Living Dead* [*Year of the Living Dead*], 2013.

CHAPTER 5: *MACBETH* AND HORROR CINEMA

Having established that *Macbeth* used the conventions of the horror genre to represent Shakespeare's play on screen, it is worth considering briefly how the film is placed in the wider historical context of the genre itself. Though it may seem incongruous at this point to start talking of films such as the Folk Horror *The Wicker Man* (1973) or slasher classic *Halloween* (1978), neither of which seems superficially to have much in common with Shakespeare or Polanski, they are worth examining. Considering how Polanski's film fits in with works such as these can show how it is situated within the history of the horror genre itself.

Having already established that, while *Rosemary's Baby* took the old conventions of the Gothic/Hammer tradition and re-imagined them for the urban landscapes of the late twentieth century, in *Macbeth*, Polanski managed to combine an eleventh-century setting and Shakespeare's poetic idiom to illustrate some very modern concerns. In addition, in the character of Ross, Polanski used Shakespeare's play to form a critique of contemporary society, exploiting and even anticipating an emerging trend in horror of the film as social commentary. This is something that has now been recognised in film academia, notably by Peter Hutchings.[1] He has traced in *Macbeth* 'a number of changes made by Polanski and his collaborators to the theatrical original' that match 'what was going on in American and British horror cinema in the late 1960s and early 1970s' (2008: 161). He identifies the shared features of *Macbeth* and films such as *Night of the Living Dead*, for example, in the re-appropriation of the Gothic tropes to create a realist approach with youthful protagonists. These young people are part of the expression of an overarching cynicism about the competence of the establishment and its institutions to serve the society they supposedly protect.

Whereas *Rosemary's Baby* could make this point more straightforwardly, being set exclusively in the present day, the realisation of the idea in *Macbeth* was achieved through the medium of Shakespeare, a text from the historical past that Polanski did not update, only adapt. His achievement in presenting modern anxieties in a setting and language remote from our own meant that the film made an impact on the horror genre in a much more subtle way that a simple rendering of new ideas through the filter of Shakespeare. What Polanski achieved in terms of the horror genre in *Macbeth* was to provide the bridge between the best of the older British Hammer tradition and the new American horrors of the 1970s.

BRITISH FOLK HORROR: *THE WICKER MAN*

This can be seen, in the first place, by the way in which, in *Macbeth*, Polanski was subconsciously absorbing a trend that was emerging from the fading glory of Hammer horror. With this decline, there were:

> ... some fascinating final flourishes. From the late Sixties the new generation of British directors avoided the Gothic cliché by stepping even further away from the modern world. Amongst these are a loose connection of films we might call 'Folk Horror'.

This was what Mark Gatiss in his television programme, *A History of Horror*, identified as a sub-genre of what he called Hammer's 'Home Counties Horror', in films such as *Witchfinder General* (1968), *The Blood on Satan's Claw* (1971) and *The Wicker Man*. This is a category that I argue should also contain Polanski's *Macbeth* which was released contemporaneously. It tends not to be regarded in this light; partly since Polanski himself has never made any explicit connection between *Macbeth* and any of the films Gatiss identifies in this category, and partly since *Macbeth* was an American production and has therefore been associated with the run of contemporary American horrors. Yet Polanski's film shares with its Folk Horror contemporaries, 'a common obsession with the British landscape, its folklore and superstitions'.[2]

Folk Horror was old horror rendered new, but not by taking any radical steps. Rather, it was achieved through the subtle realignment of the familiar in horror (the Gothic landscapes, the supernatural) with the new – an expression of the ubiquity of evil as part of the human condition. The Folk Horror films have this very much in common with *Macbeth*; and the expression of such ideas corresponds with Polanski's film. Take, for example, the 'obsession' with the landscape as it is visually presented in these films. There is a definite move away from the Hammer idea of landscape being merely a backdrop to supernatural horrors, and a new emphasis on human interaction with nature. This is present at even the most basic level – the fact that, just as with *Macbeth*, events take place almost entirely in the open air. Sergeant Howie (Edward Woodward) in *The Wicker Man* conducts his investigations largely outdoors, walking the streets and country landscapes of Summerisle. In *Witchfinder General* people are always outdoors. On the flat landscapes of Suffolk and Norfolk, Oliver Cromwell (Patrick Wymark) dines alfresco with his soldiers, people light fires, herd sheep, ride horses, fight and brawl on thick coarse grass – and drown in the water and hang from the trees.

Folk Horror films share this presentation of the landscape with *Macbeth*, even down to the opening shots. The opening scene of the sunrise in Polanski's film, the eye-pleasing shots of a vast beach and reddening sky, is akin to the opening sequence of *The Wicker Man*, where Howie's plane flies over some of the most stunning scenery in the British Isles, the aeroplane cruising over a sweeping panorama of unmistakeably Scottish glens, moors, heather, crashing waves and craggy rocks. The vistas of green and blue overshadow the small plane that flies over it illustrating that, as with *Macbeth*, landscape in Folk Horror overwhelms its inhabitants. This idea is also expressed in Piers Haggard's opening sequence of *The Blood on Satan's Claw*, which shows, in visual shorthand, all the Folk Horror landscape motifs that it shares with *Macbeth*. The first low angle shot of Ralph (Barry Andrews) ploughing the land, emphasises the diminution of the occupants of that land that is further highlighted as Ralph and Cathy (Wendy Padbury) shout greetings to one another across the field. The very fact that the film opens with Ralph ploughing illustrates another common Folk Horror motif – the use of the land for human survival.

Folk Horror films also share historical settings, part of the 'stepping away ... from the modern world' identified by Gatiss. *Witchfinder General* and *The Blood on Satan's Claw* are set in the seventeenth and eighteenth centuries respectively, a reflection of their Hammer credentials. *Macbeth* is set even earlier, in accordance with Shakespeare's play; but that film's pre-Christian setting, and thus that of the other films serves to hearken back to a time when, as we have seen, society was more dependent on the land for survival and efforts were made to tame the environment to make it habitable for humans. Folk Horror abounds with sights of the landscape being used and adapted for human survival. In *Macbeth* there are castle courtyards full of animals, and in all Folk Horror films the sight of animals is ubiquitous, with chickens, sheep, goats and cattle sharing much screen time with the human inhabitants.

In *The Wicker Man*, although it has the more modern setting, the horror manifests itself in the ongoing attempts to suborn nature to human needs. The motivation behind the pagan practices is established by Lord Summerisle (Christopher Lee) as the natural outcome of an early attempt to save a failing fruit crop and thus ensure the economic survival of the island. The inhabitants feel that they 'own' the landscape around them and can manipulate an otherwordly source to make it behave as they wish. This is directly contrasted with Howie, whose resolute Christian beliefs demand that all things are created by, and therefore under the jurisdiction of, God and that the islanders' pagan beliefs are an affront. Much of the narrative of the film centres on this contrast in beliefs. Over the course of the film, the audience watches Howie's increasing incredulity and offence at the pagan practices of the islanders without realising that in his own piety he is unwittingly becoming an accomplice.

Yet, at no point during the film are we witness to any supernatural manifestations that might support either viewpoint. The attempts to tame the landscape via the appeasement of the 'old Gods' are not verified in any way. There are no visible signs of a godly presence and neither are there any esoteric hints that such things exist. There are no manifestations to motivate the islanders; but neither are there any celestial apparitions to support Howie's beliefs that his Christian God controls the landscape. Like *Macbeth*, there is only the strength of a belief in such things, a *perception* of a numinous force that guides human actions.

Such a realisation offsets the brutality of what happens in the film's (in)famous ending. Knowing that there is no motivation behind the sacrifice of Howie other than that which the islanders have persuaded themselves is true, reflects, as does *Macbeth*, a much more brutal, chillingly matter-of-fact presentation of the human inclination to believe in non-corporeal beings that lead us to evil acts. Intriguingly, Folk Horror moves away from its Hammer predecessors in this presentation of the supernatural. In the earlier films, supernatural occurrences were, by and large, taken as real, with corporeal monsters terrorising the inhabitants of whatever sinister locality the surrounding countryside of Buckinghamshire was meant to represent; but in at least two of the Folk Horror films identified by Gatiss, the presentation of anything otherworldy is closer to the way it is in *Macbeth*. In *The Wicker Man* there are no ghosts or wraiths or visions. Supernatural forces are only *perceived* to exist.

There is no doubt in the film that Macbeth is not temporarily possessed by an evil spirit, any more than the inhabitants of Summerisle are 'raving mad', as Howie claims them to be. There are only supernatural events because the characters in these films, including Macbeth, believe that there are. In Macbeth's case, the reality for the viewer, is that he is, simply, a murderer, who only believes he has, as he says, 'a charmèd life'. Characters who deem themselves to be of great importance, are present in all Folk Horror films. There are those who consider that they have a special destiny, one that is bestowed upon them by an otherworldly source, such as Matthew Hopkins, the Witchfinder General, who has an inflated sense of his own importance, believing (or at least asserting) that he is operating for the greater good.

In *The Wicker Man* there are two men who believe that they act according to a special destiny conferred upon them by supernatural beings. Lord Summerisle acts as he does in homage to the pagan gods that he believes control the landscape that provides the islanders' living. Howie, on the other hand, believes that he is an agent of the Christian God, as well as institutional authority in his profession as police officer. His assumption of religious and moral authority is the rule of life by which he abides and is the very thing that leads to his downfall. His reiteration to the islanders of the rightness of his own beliefs and their (to him) exasperating reassurances that there is much wrongness in those beliefs is threaded throughout the film in Howie's various encounters with May Morrison (Irene Sunters), Miss Rose (Diane Cilento) and Lord Summerisle himself. Even Summerisle, who has assumed the role of island patriarch and agent of the May Day rituals, has a hint of his own vulnerability, as a frightened Howie, at the point of ritualised murder, reminds him that if the crops fail again, the islanders will come for him.

The power of the ending of *The Wicker Man*, the sight of the effigy that so terrifies Howie, is not so much in the visceral anticipation of his grisly death (though that certainly enhances the horror), but the underlying knowledge that it has come about through human and not supernatural agencies. The final shot of the wicker man engulfed in flames, knowing that it contains the charred corpse of Howie and seeing it against a truly beautiful backdrop of the glistening ocean and reddening sun is a reminder of the lengths to which humankind will go to take control of their landscapes and their destinies; and that such control is achieved through a misguided belief that it is aided by supernatural forces.

This is what makes films like *The Wicker Man* so frightening. The chill of this film, what makes it horrific, is not the sight of a ghoul or any otherworldly manifestation; but in the realisation that the origin of the horror is very much earthbound and human. It is also why Polanski's *Macbeth* works as a horror film, and, in particular, as a Folk Horror. It shares with those films the idea that what you see on the screen is not the result of an intervention with anything supernatural. It is chillingly real.

THE SLASHER FILM: *HALLOWEEN*

It might seem surprising to be talking about John Carpenter's film *Halloween* in the context of Polanski's *Macbeth*. Superficially, they have very little in common. The later film is, like *Rosemary's Baby*, set in an unmistakeably modern urban milieu, the dialogue late twentieth century, the social mores very clearly those of the post-1960s counterculture movement as opposed to the restraints of the feudal society of Medieval Scotland; but, as with *Rosemary's Baby*, it only requires a closer look at the concepts behind *Halloween* to realise that, in fact, the films have much in common. *Macbeth* can be seen to be entirely in keeping with the emerging trends in American horror epitomised by *Halloween*, which sought to explore evil as having human, social origins rather than supernatural.

This can be seen in the way *Halloween* explores the twin Folk Horror obsessions of environment and the supernatural. The twists that Folk Horror gave to the 'obsession' with British landscape and superstition were exploited by Polanski in *Macbeth*: and the same happens in *Halloween*. In *Macbeth*, Polanski used the landscape to reflect the underlying animal passions that dwelt beneath the social veneer and presented supernatural events as only being in the eye of the beholder, both characteristics of Folk Horror. In doing so, Polanski paved the way for a wider exploration of the human condition, whereby evil is seen as innate, barely hidden by the veneer of civilisation. In this way, he anticipated the trends of the later horrors of the 1970s. In Carpenter's film, this concept, that supernatural events are only a smokescreen to cover the human inclination for evil, reached its apogee.

In *Macbeth*, the film used the 'obsession' of the Folk Horror with landscape, using rural settings emphasise the primacy of nature over human concerns. In *Halloween*, there is a similar preoccupation with the landscape but the idea is taken one step further; it is not rural, it is suburban. In contrast to *Macbeth*, or *The Wicker Man* and other Folk Horror films, in *Halloween* is the sight of nature thoroughly tamed, a markedly human landscape, one that is not at all deemed to be susceptible to the ravages of nature. The streets are littered with autumn leaves (admittedly fake), but that is the only sign of anything in its natural state. Nature is otherwise shaped and tamed in manicured lawns and well-trimmed hedges – and there are no animals other than one pet dog.

This is the landscape finally shaped to accommodate human needs, epitomised by the festival after which the film is named. The very origins of Halloween itself, once an occasion dedicated to the appeasement of deities in the hope of survival in a harsh winter landscape, here is an occasion for simply having fun, removed from any need to protect the environment and ensure a productive harvest. The setting of the film itself on 31 October 1978, offers ample opportunity for Carpenter to show the folklore of the festival as translated into the twentieth-century (Leeder, 2014: 62-5), in the form of suburban divertissements. The heroine, Laurie Strode (Jamie Lee Curtis) watches children trick-or-treating, and helps them carve pumpkins into jack-o'-lanterns. That ubiquitous element of late twentieth century living, the television, is also subsumed into the Halloween entertainments, always on in the background showing re-runs of classic horror movies such as *The Thing from Another World* (1952) with a voice-over advertising their ability to spook and scare the viewer. Such intrusion into the action of the film summarises the modern approach to the old festival, not as an occasion for the superstitious habit of warding off spirits, but as an occasion of being scared for fun.

Most people in the film enjoy the occasion and participate in the festival but not in the superstition from which it evolved. At times, the approach in the film to anything supernatural is pragmatic. Tommy (Brian Andrews), whom Laurie babysits, identifies Halloween as primarily an occasion to 'get candy', but is the only character in the film who still holds on to the belief that the festival is an occasion for genuine scares. In the teasing of Tommy Doyle, we get a sense that Halloween is regarded as purely for entertainment. That he even thinks there might really be something more dangerous at its heart is summarily dismissed, mostly by Laurie. When we first see Tommy, he is meeting Laurie on her way to school and she has to drop off some keys at 'the Myers house'. Tommy tells her that she cannot approach the house since it might be haunted – 'that's a spook house' – for which she teases him. He is similarly teased by bullies at school who tell him that Halloween is when 'the boogeyman' will get him. After this, he complains that he is frightened of such a figure, but Laurie briskly dismisses any display of juvenile credulity, insisting that there is no such thing – 'It's all make believe'. When Tommy later insists that he has seen the 'Boogeyman', she blames it on the television horror marathon, reiterating firmly, 'There is no Boogeyman!'

In the imagination of Tommy there is a readiness to believe in the supernatural; but in Laurie's responses we are reminded that it is also a film in which the supernatural does not, actually, exist. Again, this might seem to distance the film even further than *Macbeth*. In that film, as in *Rosemary's Baby*, we are presented with a strong belief in the supernatural and no evidence that such a thing exists; in *Halloween* we have some very definite pronouncements that there is 'no such thing' as ghosts and boogeymen. Like *Macbeth*, we are, however, by means of clever misdirection, given hints that raise our own expectations that something supernatural is occurring, lured into a sense that the events that unfold are beyond human control. We know, for example, that Tommy is not really imagining anything – he *has* definitely seen someone through the blinds. We also know that he is right to warn Laurie against approaching the Myers house since we have seen, via a point-of-view shot, that Michael is in residence. The house itself reveals its Gothic origins as a 'haunted house', a recognisable Gothic trope, seen in splendidly ramshackle isolation. Its appearance is one of many familiar aspects of Gothic horror that have their place in showcasing to the viewer that this is a horror film. The suburban landscape is replete with the images of past horror film conventions. Ever-present darkness, ghostly white faces appearing in the windows, a damsel in distress pursued through dark corridors and hallways (albeit not in a castle), even an escaped lunatic, free to roam and kill indiscriminately according to some innate desire for destruction.

One character in particular sets the Gothic scene admirably. Dr Loomis (Donald Pleasence) is, in the film, most certainly 'an old-fashioned character seemingly visiting *Halloween* from an older mode of horror film' (Leeder, 2014: 87). When we first meet him, he is searching for Michael in a pelting rainstorm punctuated by suitably ominous rumbles of thunder and flashes of lightning. He brings the accoutrements of the Gothic landscape with him to Haddonfield. He stands outdoors surrounded by the sounds of chirruping crickets and the wind through the trees. When Tommy's bullies approach the Myers' home, he discourages their approach with a suitable imitation of a ghostly voice. His very appearance in the film evokes the old school horror of Christopher Lee and Peter Cushing.[3] He is the one at the end of the film that tells Laurie, rather flatly, that yes, despite her earlier convictions that was the 'boogeyman'; but it is only from him that we hear such things. He is the one who insists that Michael is 'the evil', even hinting that he is possessed by suggesting that something 'was living behind that boy's eyes' that 'was purely, simply evil'. Only through him do we learn that Michael has no redeeming features, no human qualities.

This idea is supported by Carpenter making Michael a half-realised creature, since he is both of the landscape and removed from it. The figure of Michael in the first part of the film is only ever seen in shadows or half-shadows, as a shape amongst features of the landscape. He is seen beside a car through a schoolroom window, emerging from a hedge, or standing in a garden, seen through the washing hanging on a line. He is seen only vaguely, on the periphery of the shot, there, and then not there. Like the women in *Macbeth*, this establishes him as an integral part of the landscape. But unlike the women, who remain in their own spaces in the film and do not intrude into the domestic interiors, Michael increasingly encroaches into the interior landscape. He enters the houses and invades the apparently safe domestic environment. That is why those final shots of the film are so scary. Even though they dwell on the human landscape of houses, hallways, landings and sofas, they still remind a viewer that the occupants of such places are human beings. And we have just seen what human beings can do.

By referring to Michael as 'The Shape' in the credits, having him dressed in a nondescript boiler suit and mask, by presenting him in shadows, filtered through the accoutrements of suburban domesticity, such as clean washing and hanging baskets, the audience is further lulled into thinking that something other-worldly is present. Yet, there is nothing supernatural happening in *Halloween*. Michael is really quite human, as we can see when Laurie tears at his mask, partially revealing a fresh-faced youth beneath; as with *Macbeth*, it is from the realisation that Michael *is* human, that the horror truly derives. It would be very comforting to have a reason why Michael does what he does, just as it is more of a consolation to think that Macbeth, too, is not in control of his actions. If their behaviour is attributable to forces outside the realms of human endeavour, it is very reassuring – to think that maybe Dr Loomis is right, maybe Michael is the personification of evil and motivated by some supernatural force. Or that maybe some weird sisters cast a ritual and he fell under their malign influence.[4]

However, the ending of *Halloween* was deliberately meant to leave Michael's motives unexplained. The central idea of the film that Carpenter wanted to convey was that there was no easy resolution, no obvious reason for Michael to do what he does. The only reason such a character is seen as being non-human is entirely due to the readings we, as viewers, impose upon him (Leeder, 2014: 96). Yet there is no such motivation – he is simply a man who kills.

In many ways this is more sinister than *Macbeth*. At least in that film, its protagonist killed to pursue his ambitions, his rise to power. There does not even seem to be that motivation for Michael; but, in common with Polanski's film is the underlying horror that there is no numinous influence on human actions. *Halloween* is *Macbeth* stripped of the distance and historical trappings to show the presence of evil as a very modern phenomenon.

FOOTNOTES

1. *Macbeth* is listed in Fenton and Flint, 2001: 111. Kim Newman mentions it as a matter of course as one of many horror films of the later twentieth century (2011: 60).
2. 'Home Counties Horror', episode 2/3. Broadcast on BBC4 on 18 October 2010.
3. Carpenter had offered them the part of Dr Loomis but both had turned it down; see the interview with Carpenter in *Birth of the Living Dead* [*Year of the Living Dead*], 2013.
4. Such a thing is hinted at in *Halloween 6: the Curse of Michael Myers* (1995) with the 'Cult of Thorn', a storyline now considered to be 'non-canonical'.

CONCLUSION

Fig. 14. Donalbain approaches the lair of the women.

At the end of *Macbeth*, after the cheers for the newly-crowned Malcolm and the sight of Macbeth's severed head pinned on a spike on the castle battlements, the scene changes. A familiar sight appears, a landscape of darkening skies, pouring rain and outcrops of craggy rock. Familiar music is heard and, from the left, a figure appears, riding toward the sound. It is Donalbain (Paul Shelley), the younger brother of Malcolm. He dismounts, and walks toward the lair of the weird sisters.

The implications of such an ending are obvious. By visiting the sisters, Donalbain signals his intent to usurp his brother. The whole story will begin again. For some Shakespeareans, this signals the film's affinity with the work of the Polish critic Jan Kott. In his *Shakespeare Our Contemporary* of 1964, Kott saw Shakespeare's Histories as representing cycles of horror whereby a route to kingship is only through crimes such as murder; and power can then only be sustained by further crimes – a view of 'history as an implacable and unending power struggle' (Rothwell, 2003: 251). It is a cycle that is inevitable since everyone is trapped in a great machine, the engine of history. Donalbain's visit to the women is a sign that he is just as trapped in this Grand Mechanism as was Macbeth.[1]

Such a reading places the film firmly in its own time, as a product of a disillusion with the Sixties countercultural idealism and the expression of a youthful anger at the collective lack of will for social change. For a Shakespearean, this ending also has one more effect. The sight of a limping, disaffected younger brother has an irresistible parallel with Shakespeare's Richard III. This might be an inadvertent association. Some commentators have considered that Donalbain's limp is not to mimic this most notable of literary icons, but 'to quickly imprint [him] in our memories, for he is permanently absent from the play after Duncan's murder' (Crowl, 1992: 24). Even so, it makes for an interesting visual parallel with Macbeth since both characters have a habit of murdering their way through a line of succession, the character of Richard bringing to mind multiple stabbings, a drowning, child murder and beheading.

The promise in Macbeth of more of the same calls to mind something else. It reminds us of the concept of the franchise – that recognisably twentieth-century phenomenon whereby a new-minted concept of the horror genre is continued in a series of sequels. Macbeth, too, is part of a franchise, not of horror, but of Shakespeare films. Much of the response to Polanski's film has been in the arena of Shakespeare studies, with the film seen as one of many ongoing adaptations of his play, one of many film interpretations of his works, which could loosely be called a franchise if we consider them to be extensions of the 'Shakespeare' brand.

Seeing another Shakespeare trademark villain in the film, a possible Richard III limping through the women's lair, also calls to mind that horror as a genre has always been with us in the theatrical medium, be it playhouse or multiplex. If we are to regard Macbeth as a part of this tradition, as one of many horror stories throughout performance history that began on the stage and developed into a discrete film genre, then the sight of the story of the film about to repeat itself calls to mind this historical continuation. It also calls to mind that smaller scale feature of the modern horror – the sequel. A promise of more of the same. After an apparent resolution in a horror film in which it seems the evil has been defeated, a further scene often shows that not to be the case – like the missing body of Michael Myers at the end of Halloween, or the sudden appearance of the disfigured Jason from the water of Camp Crystal Lake in Friday the 13th (1980). Similarly, in Macbeth, we see Donalbain reach the home of the weird women, the visit suggesting a promise of further horrors to come.

It is true that the new possibilities opened up by the endings of those films other than *Macbeth* are primarily commercial. Even if, as with *Halloween*, there was initially no intention on the part of the director of continuing the story, the financial and critical success of those films meant that for the business end of film-making, a sequel was too lucrative an opportunity to miss. This is not the only reason why sequels work, however. They are not successful just because audiences blindly stumble into the cinema at the mere indication that a film is a Toccata and Fugue away from Gothic promise. It is because the suggestion of a sequel offers so much more. Within those open endings is encapsulated the 'journey' of the film, the feeling it has evoked, the 'rollercoaster' of horror; and a promise that those emotions will continue. The anticipation of an increased cashflow might appeal to the businessmen; but for the audience there is a *frisson* of excitement, a tantalising promise of a continuation of horrors witnessed, the next rush of emotions, of thrills.

This, too, is present in *Macbeth*. We have just seen the carnage that has resulted from Macbeth's visit to the sisters and Donalbain's entry into their territory is a hint that such carnage will continue. Such a promise creates an *emotional* resonance in the audience, rather than just an intellectual one. That last emotional pull, that leaves the audience feeling a thrill at the sight of Donalbain limping around the women's lair, is why the first and lasting impression of the film is of violence and bloodshed; it brings to mind the slaughter we have just seen that was the result of Macbeth's encounter with the women. Donalbain's intrusion into their territory is a promise that such bloodshed will continue. Ending the film in this way, with the recall of all that has happened and the promise of more to come is why all of those early reviewers immediately wrote disapprovingly of the blood and violence in the film as their lasting impression. Even some of the great Shakespeareans themselves were moved by that last twang of the nerves. Kenneth S. Rothwell, one of the greats of Shakespeare film criticism, in the very first paragraph of his own response to seeing *Macbeth* in the cinema, had the impression of Golgotha, 'a place of skulls ... agony and sacrifice', and called to mind the grisly image of the old Elizabethan Hieronimo in *The Spanish Tragedy* 'biting out his own tongue and spitting it on the stage' (1973: 71).

This is because Polanski has managed to transfer the emotive power of Shakespeare's Jacobean play to film. Orson Welles and Akira Kurosawa could only treat the source play in an abstract manner, loading their films with earnest symbolism and expressionist motifs, treating Shakespeare as part-history, part-intellectual treatise. In their hands, the play actually becomes part of Shakespeare criticism, of a learned debate about Shakespeare's artistry, or historical context. Polanski's refusal to take a more abstracted approach and use the horror genre to present the play led to a film that, just as in Shakespeare's play, prompts an emotional response to its subject matter – a 'gut reaction', if you like – to the inclination of human beings to evil and the bloody consequences thereof. The play becomes, not just part of a wider field of Shakespeare criticism, but a raw-edged story of the desire for power and the ravages that ensue. Drawing them in by a variety of cinematic techniques, Polanski was able to give his audience an insight into the monstrous that lies beneath the civilised surface.

This is a subject that was deemed worthy of exploration in many horror films before and subsequently. In treating Shakespeare's play as a horror, using it to shed light on a very human preoccupation with evil and its violent and blood-spattered outcomes, Polanski anticipated the new path the genre was to take throughout the following decade. Just as in *Macbeth* Banquo holds up a series of mirrors that reflect the images of his successors that trace back to his own son Fleance, so subsequent films show their lineage to Polanski's film as their originator. With the sight of Donalbain offering a tantalising glimpse of more horrors to come, is the realisation that *Macbeth* was truly 'father to a line of kings'.

FOOTNOTES

1.   Kott's influence on staged Shakespeare has been vast and many of these productions are available on film. The most famous is Peter Brook's *King Lear*, starring Paul Scofield, staged in 1962, and released as a film just before *Macbeth* in 1971. The 2008 Royal Shakespeare Company production of *Hamlet*, released on DVD in 2009 starring David Tennant (Peter Vincent in *Fright Night* [2011]) and directed by Gregory Doran, exhibits a very Kottian preoccupation with surveillance. Ralph Fiennes (of Voldemort fame) directed and starred in *Coriolanus* (2011) which sees the title character battened by the 'grand mechanism' of history.

WORKS CITED

Ain-Kruper, Julia. *Roman Polanski: A Life In Exile*. California: ABC-CLIO, 2010.

Berlin, Normand. '*Macbeth*: Polanski and Shakespeare'. *Literature/Film Quarterly* 1 (1973): 291-8.

Birth of the Living Dead. Dir. Rob Kuhns. Matchbox Films, 2013. DVD.

Black Sunday. Dir. Mario Bava. Arrow Video, 2013. DVD/Blu-ray.

Blood on Satan's Claw. Dir. Piers Haggard. Odeon Entertainment, 2010. DVD.

Boose, Linda E. & Richard Burt. Eds. *Shakespeare, the Movie: Popularizing the Plays on Film, TV, and Video*. London: Routledge, 1997.

Brantley, Will. Ed. *Conversations with Pauline Kael*. Mississippi: Mississippi UP, 1996.

Brown, John Russell. *Macbeth*. The Shakespeare Handbooks Series. Houndmills: Palgrave, 2005.

Buchman, Lorne M. *Still In Movement: Shakespeare on Screen*. Oxford: OUP, 1991.

Bugliosi, Vincent & Curt Gentry. *Helter Skelter: The True Story of the Manson Murders*. London, W.W. Norton, 1974.

Caputo, Davide. *Polanski and Perception: The Psychology of Seeing and the Cinema of Roman Polanski*. Bristol: Intellect Books, 2012.

Cherry, Brigid. *Horror*. Routledge Film Guidebooks. Abingdon: Routledge, 2009.

Clery, E. J. 'The Genesis of "Gothic" Fiction'. *The Cambridge Companion to Gothic Fiction*. Ed. Jerrold E. Hogle. Cambridge: CUP, 2002, 21-40.

Cronin, Paul. *Roman Polanski: Interviews*. Mississippi: Mississippi UP, 2005.

Crowl, Samuel. 'Chain Reaction: A Study of Roman Polanski's "Macbeth"'. *Soundings: An Interdisciplinary Journal*. Vol 59. No. 2 (Summer 1976): 226-33.

---. *Shakespeare Observed: Studies in Performance on Stage and Screen*. Athens: Ohio UP, 1992.

Deats, Sara M. 'Polanski's Macbeth: A Contemporary Tragedy'. *Studies In Popular Culture*. Vol. 9. No. 1 (1986): 84-93.

Eagle, Herbert. 'Polanski'. *Five Filmmakers*. Ed. Daniel J. Goulding. Bloomington & Indianapolis: Indiana UP, 1994, 92-155.

Ebert, Roger. *Roger Ebert's Four Star Reviews 1967-2007*. Kansas City: Andrews McMeel, 2009.

Fenton, Harvey & David Flint. Eds. *Ten Years of Terror: British Horror Films of the 1970s*. Guilford: FAB Press, 2001.

Forsyth, Neil. 'Shakespeare the illusionist: filming the supernatural'. *The Cambridge Companion to Shakespeare on Film*. Ed. Russell Jackson. Cambridge: CUP, 280-302.

Freud, Clement. 'When Birnam Wood Went To Ffestiniog'. *Sunday Telegraph Magazine*, 5th March 1971: 32-9.

Grossvogel, David I. 'When the Stain Won't Wash: Polanski's Macbeth'. *Diacritics*. Vol. 2. No. 2 (Summer, 1972): 46-51.

Halloween. Dir. John Carpenter. Anchor Bay, 2000. DVD.

Harmes, Marcus K. *The Curse of Frankenstein*. Devil's Advocates. Leighton Buzzard: Auteur, 2015.

Hatchuel, Sarah et al. Eds. *Shakespeare on Screen: Macbeth*. Publication Univ. Rouen Havre, 2013.

A History of Horror. Dir. John Dass. BBC, October 2010.

Hulse, S. Clark. 'Wresting the Alphabet: Oratory and Action in "Titus Andronicus"'. *Criticism*. Vol 21. No. 2. (Spring, 1979): 106-18.

Hutchings, Peter. *Hammer and Beyond: the British Horror Film*. Manchester: MUP, 1993.

---. *The Horror Film*. Harlow, Essex: Pearson Education, 2004.

---. 'Theatre of Blood: Shakespeare and the Horror Film'. *Gothic Shakespeares*. Eds. John Drakakis & Dale Townshend. Abingdon: Routledge, 2008, 153-66.

Hogle, Jerrold E. 'Afterword: The "grounds" of the Shakespeare-Gothic relationship'. *Gothic Shakespeares*. Accents on Shakespeare. Eds. John Drakakis & Dale Townshend. Abingdon: Routledge, 2008, 201-20.

Jackson, Russell. 'From play-script to screenplay'. *The Cambridge Companion to Shakespeare on Film*. Ed. Russell Jackson. Cambridge: CUP, 2007, 15-34.

Jorgens, Jack J. 'The Opening Scene of Polanski's *Macbeth*'. *Literature/Film Quarterly* 3 (1975): 277-8.

---. *Shakespeare on Film*. Bloomington: Indiana UP, 1977.

Kael, Pauline. *Deeper Into Movies*. Boston: Little, Brown & Co., 1973.

King, Stephen. *Danse Macabre*. New York: Everest, 1981.

Kliman, Bernice W. 'Thanes in the Folio *Macbeth*'. *Shakespeare Bulletin* 9 (Winter 1991): 5-8.

---. 'Gleanings: the Residue of Difference in Scripts: The Case of Polanski's *Macbeth*'. *Shakespearean Illuminations: Essays in Honor of Marvin Rosenberg*. Eds. Jay L. Halio, Hugh M. Richmond & Marvin Rosenberg. London: Associated UP, 1998, 131-146.

---. *Macbeth*. Shakespeare In Performance Series. Manchester: MUP, 2004.

Macbeth. Dir. Roman Polanski. Sony Pictures Home Entertainment, 2003. DVD.

Kott, Jan. *Shakespeare Our Contemporary*. London: Methuen, 1964.

Kurosawa, Akira. *Throne of Blood*. BFI, 2001. DVD.

Leeder, Murray. *Halloween*. Devil's Advocates. Leighton Buzzard: Auteur, 2014.

Mazierska, Ewa. *Roman Polanski: The Cinema of a Cultural Traveller*. London: I. B. Tauris, 2007.

Newman, Kim. *Nightmare Movies: Horror on Screen Since the 1960s*. London: Bloomsbury, 2011.

Night of the Living Dead. Dir. George Romero. UCA, 2005. DVD.

Parker, John. *Polanski*. London: Victor Gollancz, 1993.

Pearlman, E. 'Macbeth on Film: Politics'. *Shakespeare and the Moving Image: The Plays on Film and Television*. Eds. Anthony Davies & Stanley Wells. Cambridge: CUP, 1995, 250-260.

Petersen, Per Serritslev. 'The "Bloody Business" of Roman Polanski's *Macbeth*: A Case Study of the Dynamics of Modern Shakespeare Reception'. *Screen Shakespeare*. Ed. Michael Skovmand. Aarhus: Aarhus UP, 1994, 38-53.

Polanski, Roman. *Roman*. London: Heinemann, 1984.

Rothwell, Kenneth S. 'Roman Polanski's *Macbeth*: Golgotha Triumphant'. *Literature/Film Quarterly* 1 (1973): 71-5.

---. 'Roman Polanski's *Macbeth*: the "Privileging" of Ross'. *The CEA Critic*, 46 (1983): 50-5.

---. 'Classic Film Versions of Shakespeare's Tragedies: A Mirror for the Times'. *A Companion To Shakespeare's Works*. Vol. 1 The Tragedies. Eds. Richard Dutton & Jean E. Howard. Oxford: Blackwell, 2003, 241-61.

---. *A History of Shakespeare on Screen: A Century of Film and Television*. Cambridge: CUP, 2004.

Rosemary's Baby. Dir. Roman Polanski. Paramount, 2000. DVD.

Sandford, Christopher. *Polanski*. London: Random House, 2007.

Shaefer, Dennis and Larry Salvato. *Masters of Light: Conversations with Contemporary Cinematographers*. London, California UP, 2013.

Shakespeare, William. *Macbeth*. Ed. Nicholas Brooke. Oxford World's Classics. Oxford: OUP, 1994.

Shivas, Mark. 'They're Young, They're in Love, They're the Macbeths'. *New York Times*, 28 February 1971. Sec. D: 13.

Skal, David. *The Monster Show: A Cultural History of Horror*. London: Plexus, 1994.

Wertheimer, Jürgen. 'Kurosawa's *Kumonosujo* and Polanski's *Macbeth*: Aspects of Comparative Film Criticism'. *Proceedings of the Xth Congress of the International Comparative Literature Association*. Vol. 1. Eds. Anna Balakinan et al. New York: Garland, 1985, 355-9.

Wexman, Virginia Wright. *Roman Polanski*. London: Columbus, 1987.

Williams, Deanne. 'Mick Jagger Macbeth'. *Shakespeare Survey: "Macbeth" and its Afterlife*. Vol. 57. Ed. Peter Holland. Cambridge: CUP, 2004, 145-58.

The Wicker Man. Dir. Robin Hardy. Warner, 2002. DVD.

Witchfinder General. Dir. Michael Reeves. Showbox Home Entertainment, 2007. DVD.

Wood, Robin. 'An Introduction to the American Horror Film'. *Plants of Reason: Essays on the Horror Film*. Ed. Barry Keith Grant. Metuchen, NJ: Scarecrow Press, 1984, 164-200.

Wyndham, Frances. 'The Young Macbeth', *Sunday Times Magazine*, 28 February 1971: 14-19.

Zimmerman, Paul, D. Review of Roman Polanski's "Macbeth", *Newsweek*, 10 January 1972: 59.

Zinoman, Jason. *Shock Value: How a Few Eccentric Outsiders Gave Us Nightmares, Conquered Hollywood and Invented Modern Horror*. London: Duckworth Overlook [Penguin], 2011.

Folk Horror
Hours Dreadful and Things Strange

Adam Scovell

auteur

CPSIA information can be obtained
at www.ICGtesting.com
Printed in the USA
LVOW13s1144170317
527583LV00004B/7/P